"That new dyslexic student in our school is allergic to peanuts, carries an EpiPen 24/7, and had an IEP last year. If he goes into an anaphylactic shock in class next week, what should I have done differently? What if his reading comprehension level continues to fall compared to his peers? Am I, my school, and my school district liable for harm? To prevent these fears and scenarios from becoming your reality, read this book."

Peter W. D. Wright, *Attorney at Law*

"Dr. Joanne Lane has woven federal and state special education laws into the fabric of school routines, preparing leaders and teachers on how best to avoid non-compliance. Using the format of the school calendar, Dr. Lane highlights common areas of neglect while suggesting ways to enhance the educational experience of students with special needs. Every educator must have this well-written book on their desk to address organizational preparation, parental communications, and emergency situations that could save the lives of our precious students."

Jan P. Hammond, Ed.D., *Professor Emerita,*
State University of New York at New Paltz, NY

"This go to handbook is exactly what the special education practitioner needs. Dr. Lane has cleverly created a step-by-step guide that is almost fail safe. I can see this being especially helpful to the new director or administrator of a special education program. As a former Director of Special Education, I can say with confidence that this handbook would have been exceedingly helpful."

Josephine Moffett, Ed.D., *Director of the Executive*
Leadership Ed.D. Program for St. John Fisher University

"This practical book is very useful for all Education Leaders not just Special Education specialists. There are children with special needs in every school and all building and district leaders should be aware of the cycle of requirements. The format is perfect and reflects the issues as they come up throughout the year."

Rose Rudnitski, Ed.D., *Professor and Program Director*
in Educational Leadership, Mercy University, New York

"I am the father of a child with an IEP and three disabilities. It has been all too apparent in the negative experiences my child has endured that school administrators lack an understanding of special education and are disconnected from their responsibilities in managing related issues.

This book can be a constructive guide for them to develop insight, an understanding of special education law and their accountability in addressing the needs of students with disabilities."

Tim McArdle, *Parent*

"Dr. Lane has recognized the impact of administrative misconceptions of IDEA on day-to-day, month to month and yearly school operations. Her easy-to-follow guide outlines the required special education benchmarks in a logical order and provides budgetary, personnel, and programmatic suggestions so general and special education can work together for the benefit of all students. As a building leader, it provides the true Big Picture of the year, decreasing unexpected or unplanned-for expenses and events. It supports legal compliance, but equally as important, it empowers the reader. Shared knowledge can only assist in building a strong partnership between building and pupil personnel administrators, so all students are OUR students."

Rebecca Green, *Executive Director of Educational Resources, Dutchess BOCES*

"Dr. Lane's book, *The Principal's Special Education Calendar*, is an indispensable resource for school leaders. As a former principal and director of elementary education, I can attest to its practicality and relevance. This month-by-month guide equips principals with the essential knowledge and strategies needed to ensure consistency, equity and compliance in special education, making it a must have for any school striving for excellence."

Paula C. Perez, Ed.D., *Former Principal and Director of Elementary Education, Kingston City Schools*

"I have known Dr. Lane for many years and can attest first-hand to her formidable and unique talents. Principals are responsible for the learning needs of all students. This particular text is geared to the most vulnerable of those students and provides a framework that guarantees success. It is easy to follow, time-lined and succinct. The book is deeply informative, and an astute guideline borne of exceptional academic and practical experience."

Al Derry, *Former School Superintendent, Sullivan West CSD*

The Principal's Special Education Calendar

The Principal's Special Education Calendar is a pragmatic, "do-now" guide that addresses a building leader's special education responsibilities over the course of the school year.

Developed for novice and experienced principals, it also meets the needs of professors and aspiring principal candidates looking for a resource to bridge theoretical approaches with the practical aspects of the job.

Based on quarterly marking periods for ease of planning and organization, this book provides a comprehensive guide for principals. It includes real-life scenarios, legal red flags, must-have resources to illustrate "Why this is important," and key monthly tasks with concluding checklists that recap the top action items for follow-up—all in a conversational, easy-to-read format.

With a focus on what information principals need to know, when to know it, and why, this book is the ultimate hands-on special education guide for principals everywhere to build compliance and fill in the gaps left bare in preparation programs.

Joanne W. Lane, Ed.D., is a former school administrator with more than forty years of experience in K–12 settings and higher education as a speech-language pathologist, principal, director of special education, assistant superintendent, adjunct lecturer, and internship supervisor in educational administration. She currently serves as a special education consultant in New York State.

Also Available from Routledge Eye on Education
(www.routledge.com/K-12)

Creative Sound Play for Young Learners: A Teacher's Guide to Enhancing Transition Times, Classroom Communities, SEL, and Executive Function Skills
Hayes Greenfield

Redesigning Special Education Systems through Collaborative Problem Solving: A Guidebook for School Leaders
Michelle Brenner, Kelly Miller

How to Better Serve Racially, Ethnically, and Linguistically Diverse (RELD) Students in Special Education: A Guide for Under-resourced Educators and High-needs Schools
Buruuj Tunsill

The Participatory Creativity Guide for Educators
Edward P. Clapp, Julie Rains

Disability in the Family: Guidance for Professionals from Parents and Guardians
Barbara Boroson

The Principal's Special Education Calendar

A Month-by-Month Roadmap to Building Consistency, Equity, and Compliance in Your School

Joanne W. Lane

Routledge
Taylor & Francis Group

NEW YORK AND LONDON

Designed cover image: getty images

First published 2025
by Routledge
605 Third Avenue, New York, NY 10158

and by Routledge
4 Park Square, Milton Park, Abingdon, Oxon, OX14 4RN

Routledge is an imprint of the Taylor & Francis Group, an informa business

Library of Congress Cataloging-in-Publication Data
Names: Lane, Joanne W., author.
Title: The principal's special education calendar : a month-by-month roadmap to building consistency, equity, and compliance in your school / Joanne W. Lane.
Description: New York, NY : Routledge, 2025. | Series: Routledge eye on education | Includes bibliographical references.
Identifiers: LCCN 2024029612 (print) | LCCN 2024029613 (ebook) | ISBN 9781032774305 (hardback) | ISBN 9781032771632 (paperback) | ISBN 9781003483045 (ebook)
Subjects: LCSH: Special education--United States--Planning. | Special education--United States--Administration. | Special education--Standards--United States. | School principals--United States.
Classification: LCC LC4031 .L337 2025 (print) | LCC LC4031 (ebook) | DDC 371.90973--dc23/eng/20240826
LC record available at https://lccn.loc.gov/2024029612
LC ebook record available at https://lccn.loc.gov/2024029613

ISBN: 978-1-032-77430-5 (hbk)
ISBN: 978-1-032-77163-2 (pbk)
ISBN: 978-1-003-48304-5 (ebk)

DOI: 10.4324/9781003483045

Typeset in Palatino
by KnowledgeWorks Global Ltd.

This book is dedicated to all principal leaders who embrace the value of inclusivity and work to create an environment where all students with disabilities are supported, celebrated, and empowered to reach their fullest potential.

Contents

List of Tables

Preface

It's no secret that the day-to-day realities of a principal's job may not align with the curriculum studied in preparation. Research confirms that most educational leadership programs preparing candidates to assume building-level administrative positions have a partial blind spot when it comes to special education. But with over 7.5 million classified students aged 3–21, which is a number on the rise, and the growing discussion on social justice leadership and inclusive schooling practices, the lack of focus is concerning—because *you* are in the hot seat.

Many of you might transition into the principalship from a general education background and be tempted to think, "We have a director of special education; isn't that *their* job?" However, both roles are integrated because your program delivery and service provision systems are linked. You also share professional accountability to ensure students receive the necessary supports for academic success, and both of you, in addition to your faculty, staff and school district, risk potential liability when things go awry. Acknowledging the gap in leadership preparation, *The Principal's Special Education Calendar: A Month-by-Month Roadmap to Building Consistency, Equity, and Compliance in Your School* offers a practical guidebook to help you navigate the diverse aspects of special education as the building leader in an easy-to-follow, conversational format.

This resource aims to address common misconceptions or comments from teachers, building administrators, or internship candidates, such as, "Why can't I just schedule the special education classes to go as a group to specials? It's easier that way," "Why can't I just pull the aide? It's not a big deal for two periods," or "Special education kids shouldn't get the building level remediation because they're already getting services. I need to leave those services for *my* general education kids." Thinking about those comments brought back memories of being a CSE chairperson when, while observing a student on the playground at recess, an administrator walked up to me and said, "What are you going to do about *your* kids?" Wow—I always operated under the premise that they were *our* kids. Comments such as these over the course of more than forty years in education planted the seed for this book.

While primarily intended for school principals and assistant principals, both experienced and new, the book also offers valuable insights for district leaders, internship candidates, and professors in educational administration programs. It bridges the gap between theoretical knowledge and practical application, encouraging the enhancement of current practices and the development of more inclusive leadership approaches. It provides a broad-based view of the nuances involved in areas such as programming, adherence to regulations, the importance of a defined curriculum, and a systems-based leadership approach against the backdrop of the school year. Drawing from my background in education, including as a principal, director of special education, and adjunct lecturer, this book serves as a roadmap toward the creation of consistency of operation, equality of treatment, and legal compliance under the umbrella of "Special education and doing what's right for kids."

Acknowledgments

One doesn't reach this point in the journey alone.

This book is the result of many conversations with school administrators, former students, internship candidates, and parents of students with disabilities, which revealed a critical knowledge gap in leadership preparation in special education.

To my colleagues and friends, your thoughtful feedback helped clarify and shape my ideas.

Thanks also to Joyce Long, whose experiences in both special education and school administration provided varied perspectives and relevance to the topics.

The peer review feedback received from distinguished professors Jan P. Hammond, Ed.D., Rose Rudnitski, Ed.D., and Devon Duhaney, Ed.D., and the expert in the field, Peter W. D. Wright, Attorney at Law, was invaluable in supporting the central premise of this book.

To the skillful team at Routledge, thank you for your expertise in successfully bringing this book to completion, and to Alexis O'Brien, editor, who understood my vision from the start.

Finally, thank you to my husband Ray, for his unwavering support and words of encouragement throughout this journey; to my son Ian, for his enthusiastic editorial input and boundless suggestions; and to my daughter Tracy, who insisted that if she could finish her doctoral thesis, I could certainly finish this book.

About the Author

Dr. Joanne W. Lane is a former school administrator with more than forty years of experience within K–12 settings and higher education as a certified speech-language pathologist, principal, director of special education, assistant superintendent for student support services, adjunct lecturer, and internship supervisor in educational administration.

Her programs and training materials have been recognized by the New York State Education Department as exhibiting best practices. She has been a speaker at multiple professional conferences, held board positions in community and professional organizations, and served as Vice President for Community and Affiliate Relations for the New York State Association for Supervision Curriculum Development, as well as the President of the Mid-Hudson affiliate of NYSASCD. Dr. Lane is also a member of the Association for Supervision Curriculum and Development (ASCD), School Administrators Association of New York State (SAANYS), and the Council for Exceptional Children (CEC), inclusive of the following special interest divisions: Council of Administrators of Special Education (CASE) and the Division of International Special Education Services (DISES).

She is the recent recipient of the Irving Schwartz Distinguished Retiree Award from the School Administrators Association of New York State.

Dr. Lane received her Ed.D. in Education Leadership, Management, and Policy from Seton Hall University and currently serves as a special education consultant in New York State.

Introduction

Format of This Book

This book is divided into five parts, beginning with a summer planning itinerary, and designed around the school calendar's four quarter marking periods as detailed in the table of contents. Each section outlines particular aspects of special education to address monthly, culminating with key focus areas for the quarterly report cards issued in November, February, April and June, including the five-week progress reports for review.

This approach is beneficial for school principals as it provides a comprehensive overview of special education activities before and after your appointment, thus allowing you to see the bigger picture and plan accordingly. The structure also helps in understanding the timeline and context of your responsibilities throughout the academic year. While some entries can be delegated, each one is essential as it builds upon prior activities or prepares for upcoming ones. You may observe some repetition in the chapter contents, albeit with different tasks assigned. This is intentional to highlight the importance of maintaining focus on these areas throughout the year.

Each chapter is based on the document *PSEL 2015 and Promoting Principal Leadership for the Success of Students with Disabilities* by the Council of Chief State School Officers (CCSSO) and the Collaboration for Effective Educator Development, Accountability, and Reform Center (CEEDAR, 2017). The following professional standards for educational leaders are identified monthly by their corresponding number, will vary depending on the tasks for that month, and focus on inclusive leadership practices:

1. Mission, Vision, and Core Values
2. Ethics and Professional Norms

3. Equity and Cultural Responsiveness
4. Curriculum, Instruction, and Assessment
5. Communities of Student Care and Support
6. Professional Capacity of School Personnel
7. Professional Community for Teachers and Staff
8. Meaningful Engagement of Families and Community
9. Operations and Management
10. School Improvement

Each entry is followed by a section titled, "Why is this important?" that explains the necessity of the task and supported by references to the Individuals with Disabilities Education Act (IDEA) or other relevant regulations as needed. The book provides recommendations on how to deliver identified activities, a master calendar, supplemental resources and real-world examples to both inform and guide your thinking as you progress through each month, which concludes with a checklist of follow-up tasks and references (if indicated) before moving on.

How to Use This Book

Although the sections are structured in a quarterly marking period format, they can easily be adapted to a trimester schedule based on your district's school calendar. Keep in mind that the order of contents presented in each chapter is not intended to be carried out precisely in sequence but as a guide to what is generally covered that month, given the progression of special education functions throughout the year. They can be adjusted according to your practice and the district's processes, and you can delegate them as you deem necessary.

Utilize this book as a resource to bridge a theory–practice gap in your leadership program or to further inform how to navigate your internship experience. Post the list of monthly activities on your bulletin board or place it in a tickler file for reference. Share them with your assistant principal and secretary as a form of checks and balances so that all are aware of special education areas of focus for the month. Collaborate with the director of special education to develop a cohesive list that aligns with procedures currently in place and/or discuss options for change.

Building capacity among faculty and staff and fostering a collaborative culture are vital components to your role as the instructional leader and in creating a supportive and effective special education environment. Use the information presented to develop your roadmap toward understanding and inclusivity. You may take detours, pause because some sections are under construction, hit some bumps along the way, or have a longer wait time to get to your destination, but you *will* arrive—and your students, faculty, and staff (as well as your parents) will reap the benefits.

Note: The term *director of special education* also implies director of pupil personnel services, director of student support services, or a similar term utilized in your district.

Disclaimer: This book is for information and educational purposes only. Moreover, although some scenarios throughout the book are based on real events, the names, characteristics, and identifying details have been changed to protect the privacy of individuals.

Part I
Summer Planning

1

July

The following principal leadership standards support your tasks for this month.

Box 1.1 2015 PSEL and Promoting Principal Leadership for the Success of Students with Disabilities

Effective principals …

(2) adhere to professional norms and possess an ethical mindset as they manage the dilemmas that can arise in supporting students with disabilities and promote said behaviors among faculty and staff.

(5) build a safe, caring, and healthy environment for students with disabilities that promotes inclusivity and opportunities to learn from their non-disabled peers to the greatest extent possible.

(6) provide high-quality, meaningful, professional development to effectively educate students with disabilities.

(9) manage their budgets; assign roles and responsibilities to optimize staff capacity to address each student's learning needs; manage school structures, operations, and administrative systems to support students with disabilities; and know, comply with, and help the school community understand local, state and federal laws, rights, policies, and regulations so as to promote student success.

DOI: 10.4324/9781003483045-2

Communities of Student Care and Support

Individual Education Program—Special Alerts

♦ Speak with the school nurse and the director of special education to determine how respective faculty and staff, possibly bus drivers (on a need-to-know basis) will be notified of students who have special health care needs, generally listed under Special Alerts on the IEP or in the Physical Development section.

Why Is This Important?

Health concerns vary from bee stings and peanut allergies, migraines, juvenile rheumatoid arthritis, and diabetes to medically fragile (e.g., feeding tube, ventilator assisted, etc.). Students may wear hearing aids and have FM equipment for school use. Ask if any staff training is needed to administer medical intervention in an emergency. Be sure to invite the athletic coaches (possibly the school physician) as specific plans may be needed including determining the nearest hospital to the event site, how to manage the student's medical issue in the interim, contact numbers for parent/guardian on days of athletic meets, field trips, etc. Depending on the health care plan, have the student's parents been asked to address their child's medical issues at a meeting?

Knowledge of and prompt attention to addressing any medical concerns is vital to the health and well-being of students to ensure their safety as well as the safety of others. This is also why it is critical to develop a plan that addresses how to manage the health office and students' medical needs in the absence of a school nurse. Processes like ensuring scripts are on file for all Processes like ensuring scripts are on file for all medication being dispensed and medicine bottles properly labeled are necessary. For example, a Ziploc bag containing loose medication with the name of the student written on it in magic marker or stored in a repurposed aspirin bottle will not suffice. We take it for granted that every school has a school nurse, but that is not always the case. As a principal, you could suddenly be placed in a position of having to administer medication to students. How do you manage a student with epilepsy? In diabetic shock? A flare-up of juvenile rheumatoid arthritis? A plan of action is essential and should be reviewed yearly as students' medical needs change.

Professional Capacity of School Personnel

Professional Development Plans

◆ Do the professional development plans for your building integrate with plans the director of special education is considering for the school year, or prior to the start of school?

Why Is This Important?

The professional development plans for your district may have been predetermined. However, if this planning occurs during the summer months, the closer you align your building-level training between your special educators and general educators, the greater the cohesiveness and working relationship between the two parties. Consider professional development in areas such as the importance of utilizing pre-referral strategies (e.g., Response to Intervention), progress monitoring techniques, understanding student classifications under the Individuals with Disabilities Education Act (IDEA) and best practices for instruction.

Operations and Management

Summer School Preparation

◆ Obtain a list of students with IEPs and 504 plans attending your building's summer school program, as that program is open to all students. These students are entitled to receive supports and accommodations as noted on their IEP.

◆ A building-wide summer school program is *not* to be confused with extended school year (ESY) services, which is a continuation of special education and related services for students with disabilities (as stipulated on their IEP) to prevent/minimize regression of learned skills (34 C.F.R. § 300.106[a][1]).

◆ Follow up with your school nurse to confirm they are aware of any specific medical concerns for students attending summer school.

◆ Ask your director of special education if a system is in place to verify that teachers have viewed the IEPs or 504 plans of students in attendance given the instructional focus for summer school intervention.

◆ Do any students require assistive technology tools to access the summer school program?

Why Is This Important?

Your summer school teachers should be cognizant of students in attendance who have IEPs or 504 plans to allow them the opportunity to differentiate instruction where necessary. Since students are still entitled to receive their supports and accommodations (including any assistive technology tools), check with your director of special education that this is in place and all IEPs and 504 plans are finalized, uploaded, and visible— at the very least, for your summer school students. Assuming the assistant principal will continue to handle any disciplinary issues during summer school, they should be aware of possible student concerns, hence the importance of scheduling a meeting prior to the start of the program to discuss any particular student needs or issues.

Summer weather brings another variable for medical reasons, such as asthma, bee stings, and allergies. Just like during the school year, the nurse must be conscious of any health-related special alerts on IEPs or 504 plans, and which students require assistance with dispensing medication, are supervision only, or are independent in self-administering.

Assistive Technology Needs

◆ Contact the director of special education for a list of students in your building who require assistive technology for the new school year as mandated by their individualized education plan (IEP). Assistive technology takes many forms. By law, it is "any item, piece of equipment, or product system, whether acquired commercially off the shelf, modified, or customized, that is used to increase, maintain, or improve the functional capabilities of a child with a disability" (20 U.S.C. § 1401[1][A]). Examples run the gamut from low-tech to high-tech, including slant boards, pencil grips, hearing aids, wheelchairs, crutches, dictation software, and communication devices.

◆ Inquire of the related services providers assigned to your building (e.g., occupational therapist, physical therapist, speech therapist, teacher of the deaf and hard of hearing) if teacher training will be needed to appropriately use the specific types of equipment/tools of students in their caseload.

◆ Confirm with your director of technology that identified classrooms can accommodate students' devices and particular software needs.

Why Is This Important?

Section 508 of the Rehabilitation Act of 1973 (29 U.S.C. § 798) mandates that electronic and information technology (EIT) utilized by federal agencies are accessible to individuals with disabilities regardless of the mode of delivery (e.g., computers, tablets, keyboards, content on websites, assistive technology, use of screen readers, closed captions, etc.), hence the conversation with your director of technology. If professional development will be needed prior to the start of the school year, discuss this with your director of special education to determine how best to arrange for this training (e.g., through an outside consultant, internal staff member, or a cooperative service [Co-Ser] with a neighboring agency or district). Maintain an awareness of students who have defined physical needs that fall under assistive technology, especially in emergency situations.

Box 1.2 Assistive Technology Scenario

Problem: You have to hold an emergency evacuation and need to get all students out of the building in a hurry. A student who is able to travel independently with their wheelchair happened to stop to go to the bathroom down the hallway on their way back from delivering a note to the cafeteria. The teacher does a count outside and realizes that in their haste to leave the building, they are missing this student. How can you address this situation to avoid a reoccurrence?

Outcome: Your building should have an emergency preparedness plan as part of the district-wide Wellness plan. The building plan would include a list of responsibilities for identified faculty/staff during an evacuation (e.g., Who checks the bathrooms on each floor?). Also having accessible seating (e.g., evacuation chairs) at a stairwell would be required if that is part of the evacuation route for students who would otherwise need to take the elevator during an emergency.

New Entrants Transitioning from Services Under the Committee on Preschool Education

♦ Contact the CPSE/CSE chairperson or the director of special education for a current list of any preschool students with a disability (PSD) who are "Turning 5" and eligible to enter kindergarten in September (pending your district's cutoff for kindergarten). These are students who were recommended to continue receiving special education services under the Committee on Special Education (CSE).

Why Is This Important?

The update will provide you with the necessary information to adjust your kindergarten enrollment and assess if you need to create a new section or make room facilitation changes (e.g., a student may need a classroom with bathroom access, near the nurse's office for medical reasons, or possibly in a class farthest from the exit if there are elopement concerns). Discuss any concerns with the director of special education.

Furthermore, it is important to look at the services these students are receiving to identify if they are being provided as push-in or pull-out. How many adults will be in/out of the classroom? Do any of these students have teacher aide/assistant support for all or part of the day? It is not uncommon for kindergarten students to receive push-in supports from related service providers (e.g., speech therapist, direct consultant teacher, etc.) or assistance from an aide if recommended by the CSE. An awareness of the number of adults providing in-classroom support will be helpful as you *may* experience dissension in the ranks because of it.

The underlying concern is that other kindergarten teachers also have little ones with needs such as help tying shoes, opening juice boxes, putting on coats, staying on task, etc. (but no students with IEPs). With creativity, you may be in a position to offer some assistance. This may come from a rotation in your staff schedules, parent volunteers, or older students for brief periods (even if just to read a book at circle time). You may be able to adjust the enrollments to try and distribute the services and support, but because of student requirements and/or groupings, this may not be possible. Nonetheless, it is essential to address this situation up front to avoid any underlying friction in order to create a more supportive and inclusive environment for all.

Student Enrollment and Integrated Co-Teaching Ratios

◆ Though class lists have already been determined, not all IEPs may have been finalized by June, especially if CPSE "Turning 5" meetings or transfer student CSE meetings are occurring during the summer months. Continue to monitor your class enrollment numbers.

Why Is This Important?

Special education is a fluid process. Staying informed is critical for adjusting class sizes, faculty and staff assignments, room placements, etc. Review the teacher contract language as it may have a clause indicating how much advance notice needs to be given if there is a change in teaching assignment.

Of consideration is the ratio of special education students to general education students in a classroom, as this can impact class sections and teacher assignments. In New York State, the guideline is to have no more than 12 students with a disability in an integrated co-teaching class (8 C.R.R.-NY § 200.6[g][1] [i]-[ii]). If necessary, your director of special education can increase the ratio by two additional students (under specified conditions) by applying to your state education department for prior approval of a variance. Note that some students may be placed in the integrated co-teaching class or special class for one subject or a portion of the school day. For example, a student may have integrated co-teaching for English, science, and social studies but be placed in a 12:1:1 special class for math given their need for additional support; therefore, your integrated co-teaching student numbers with IEPs is 11 vs. 12 for that particular math period when the student is not in the class. This is an important consideration when class sizes are usually capped by the board of education policy or federal law.

Be sure to familiarize yourself with the rules in your state, as your co-teaching ratios may differ. For example, the regulations might say that class size depends on the number of students with disabilities *in a particular grade*. In this case, a percentage will be applied to determine the ratio per class.

Maintaining a balance in your student enrollment is critical to ensuring a diverse and inclusive learning environment. Exercise caution not to create a de facto special education class by virtue of your enrollment as well. By staying informed, you maintain an awareness of which classes to place new entrants in as they register for school over the summer months.

Box 1.3 Integrated Co-Teaching Student Ratio Scenario

Problem (NYS): You have a teacher assistant in your integrated 3rd grade co-teaching class and two new entrants with IEPs for a similar grade/class. You already have 12 students with IEPs in the class, but only seven have integrated co-teaching on their IEP. Can you utilize the teaching assistant as a quasi-special education teacher to accommodate these two new entrants?

Outcome (NYS): The maximum number of students with disabilities that you can have in an integrated co-teaching class in NYS is 12 (8 C.R.R.-NY § 200.6[g][1]). The 12 students include *any* student with a disability, regardless of whether they were recommended for integrated co-teaching or not. For example, three students were recommended for resource room, two for speech therapy, and seven students had integrated co-teaching listed on their IEP; however, you must count the *total* of 12 students for the integrated co-teaching class, which means you have reached the maximum number of students with disabilities for that class. The teacher assistant cannot serve as a quasi-special education teacher to deliver initial instruction in order to increase enrollment, so other accommodations need to be made for the new entrants.

Responsibilities of Teacher Aides and Teacher Assistants in Special Education

  ◆ Are you aware of the differences between teacher aides and teacher assistants in terms of assignment and job responsibilities for September?

Why Is This Important?

Understanding the roles and responsibilities of your teacher aides and assistants in special education is important for being prepared in case of any emergent situations. Teacher aides primarily handle noninstructional tasks such as assisting with a student's physical needs, support for redirection, or orientation and mobility, while teacher assistants are able to carry out instructional duties like reteaching and collecting student data under the guidance of a certified teacher.

Some teacher aides may be designated as 1:1 aides according to a student's IEP, meaning they are responsible for supporting a single student either for the entire school day or part of it. Detailed criteria for determining a student's need for a 1:1 aide and the aide's responsibilities can be found on the New York State Education Department (NYSED) website under Special Education, but check your state's education website for guidelines in this area.

Having a copy of their schedules and assignments will help you identify the availability of support in case of emergencies elsewhere in the school. This knowledge enables you to reassign staff appropriately while staying compliant with students' IEPs.

Box 1.4 FAPE Scenario

Problem: "We were shy a cafeteria aide in the lunchroom for two periods, so I reassigned the 1:1 aide from Ryan because they were at Art and then going to the computer lab for Technology. I figured that because the classes were not one of their four core subjects, it would be fine. Ryan's mother stopped in to see me the next day, very upset because they were to have aide coverage for the full day in school. She said she had the right to file a complaint with the state regional associate because I did not follow Ryan's IEP. Can she do that?"

Outcome: Yes, she can contact the state regional associate assigned to your school district to complain. It violates the IEP to remove a teacher aide/assistant from a student or groups of students (such as in an integrated co-teaching class) if adult support is listed as a necessary accommodation. Advocates and attorneys will view this as impacting the student's ability to fully access their academic program, and you risk a formal complaint for denying the student a free appropriate public education (FAPE).

Transfer Students with an IEP or 504 Plan

◆ Stay informed of transfer students with IEPs or 504 plans registering during the summer months as the increase may skew your course enrollment numbers and have further implications regarding the need for additional services and support.

Why Is This Important?

If the CSE transfer meeting or 504 meeting is held during the summer, you can make the necessary program and/or staffing adjustments before the start of the school year; otherwise, changes may be necessary once the year begins as the CSE or 504 team may recommend new services and accommodations.

When the new school year begins, note that federal regulations take precedence over teacher contractual agreements which may state that they are to have a specific period of time (e.g., 48 hours) before a new student with an IEP joins their class. It is advantageous to notify your teachers to set aside additional materials as a contingency plan for unexpected student arrivals.

Student Management System—Access to IEPs and 504 Plans

◆ Substantiate that students' IEPs and 504 plans are visible in your student management system.

◆ What is the process to ensure that teachers have viewed students' IEPs and 504 plans?

Why Is This Important?

Ensuring that students' IEPs and 504 plans are accessible is essential for providing them with the necessary supports and accommodations as per a free appropriate public education (FAPE).

Chapter 408 of the New York State Education Law stipulates that each teacher and service provider who is responsible for implementing a student's IEP has electronic access or a hard copy. Districts can create a chapter 408 signature form for verification. For those who use an electronic system like School Tool, teachers can access students' IEPs and 504 plans by logging in to their class account and providing an electronic signature for verification.

Confirm with your director of special education that a process is in place to prevent any issues and ensure accountability. This not only benefits the students but also helps schools stay compliant with regulations and avoid potential legal complications.

Box 1.5 IEP Awareness Scenario

Problem: Logan did not get their test accommodations for the biology regents and failed it. Logan's father called to complain and reported that the teacher said they were unaware that test accommodations were listed on the IEP. "Was I supposed to know that, much less tell the teacher?"

Outcome: You do not need to know Logan's specific test accommodations; however, you do need to ensure that all teachers have access to the information and are aware. A reminder email at the start of the school year would also be beneficial.

New York State School Safety and Educational Climate Report

- ◆ Review the report with a designated team (and include the Dignity for All Students Act [DASA] coordinator, who may also be you as the school principal if employed as a school leader in New York State), and identify any incidents that included classified students.
- ◆ Include the Building Leadership Team (BLT), or a representative, in the meeting if such a committee exists in your school.

Why Is This Important?

The NYS School Safety and Educational Climate (SSEC) report includes both the data on violent and disruptive incidents (formerly known as VADIR), and the NYS Dignity for All Students Act (DASA), which documents incidents of discrimination, harassment, bullying, and cyberbullying. Analyzing the data to identify trends will help determine any necessary adjustments to the school-wide behavior program, such as Positive Behavioral

Interventions and Supports (PBIS) or Responsive Classroom. This may also involve revising the Code of Conduct or implementing restorative practices.

Refer to your state's education department for a similar report, albeit under a different title (e.g., School Environmental Safety Incident Reporting [SESIR] in Florida). Note that individual states have the authority to establish their own standards for assessing and comparing levels of violence among schools.

July Checklist

Did you ...

- ☐ confirm the number of students with IEPs and 504 plans for summer school?
- ☐ speak with the director of special education about aligning professional development plans, and a process for teacher verification of IEPs and 504 plans?
- ☐ request a list of assistive technology needs?
- ☐ obtain schedules for summer CSE and "Turning 5" CPSE meetings?
- ☐ follow up on IEP special alerts/medical needs with the school nurse and director of special education?
- ☐ review your class enrollment sizes to ensure legal compliance with integrated co-teaching class ratios in your state?
- ☐ obtain a copy of the teacher aide/assistant schedules and assignments?
- ☐ verify the programs of transfer students with IEPs or 504 plans to monitor class enrollment?
- ☐ speak with the director of technology about assistive technology needs and compatibility with current resources?
- ☐ notice any patterns in the School Safety and Educational Climate report regarding students with IEPs or 504 plans and develop a plan for addressing?
- ☐ review the budget to assess if additional funds are needed to cover possible costs for increases in human and/or material resources?

References

Individuals with Disabilities Education Act of 2004, 20 U.S.C. 1401 (2019). https://sites.ed.gov/idea/statute-chapter-33/subchapter-i/1401/1

IDEA Regulations, 34 C.F.R. § 300.106 (2024). https://sites.ed.gov/idea/regs/b/b/300.106

New York State Education Law, § 4402, as amended by Chapter 408 of the Laws of 2002 (2022). https://www.nysed.gov/sites/default/files/programs/special-education/nys-608-analysis.pdf

Section 508 of the Rehabilitation Act of 1973, 29 U.S.C. § 798 (2017). https://www2.ed.gov/policy/gen/guid/assistivetech.html

State of New York. Commissioner of Education. (2024). *Part 200 of the Regulations of the Commissioner.* New York State Education Department. https://www.nysed.gov/special-education/section-2006-continuum-services

2

August

The following principal leadership standards support your tasks for this month.

Box 2.1 PSEL 2015 and Promoting Principal Leadership for the Success of Students with Disabilities

Effective leaders ...

(3) ensure equitable access to effective teachers; provide culturally responsive learning opportunities, academic and social support, and other resources necessary for success; develop policies to address student misconduct in an unbiased manner; and confront and alter institutional biases of student marginalization.

(5) build a safe, caring, and healthy environment for students with disabilities that promotes inclusivity.

(7) establish a sense of collective responsibility and mutual accountability for the success of students with disabilities.

(8) create partnerships with families of students with disabilities through public and private sectors to support student learning in and out of school.

DOI: 10.4324/9781003483045-3

(9) manage school structures, operations, and systems to support students with disabilities; know, comply with, and help the school community understand local, state, and federal laws, rights, policies, and regulations so as to promote student success.

(10) establish an imperative for improvement by emphasizing the "why" and "how" of change.

Equity and Cultural Responsiveness

English Language Learners with a Handicapping Condition

◆ Students in this category will require two levels of support—that of the ENL teacher to address their level of English proficiency and alignment to IEP goals, and specialized instruction delivered by the special education teacher (possibly other related services providers such as the speech therapist).

◆ They can also be provided building-level supports (AIS, RTI, MTSS).

Why Is This Important?

It is always a challenge when students enter who are limited English proficient and their needs are variable. For example, I had a new entrant enroll just a few weeks before the administering of state exams who required an interpreter fluent in a specific dialect in Tongan. Fortunately, I was able to find an individual who resided in the area and met the necessary criteria … it was serendipitous. While knowing this information beforehand is beneficial, it is impractical since new students enroll at various times throughout the year.

From a planning perspective, speak with the director of special education to inquire if financial resources are available to address the ELL population in your school, potentially through the federal grant, Title III Part A, also known as English Language Acquisition, Language Enhancement, and

Academic Achievement Act (20 U.S.C. 6825 § 3115[d][1][2]). Monies can be used to contract for interpreters, upgrade instructional and assessment materials, educational technology (e.g., translator applications to support communication and accommodate linguistic differences for non-English speaking students), parent and family outreach, etc.

Providing an avenue for parent/guardian input and oversight of their child's special education program is a foundational aspect of IDEA 2004. The Elementary and Secondary Education Act (20 U.S.C. 6312 § 1112[e][4]) also stipulates that schools must provide information to parents in an understandable and uniform format, and to the extent practicable, in a language they can understand. Working together with your ENL teacher and director of special education will ensure that everyone is informed about the actions needed to support your ELL students in their instructional programs.

Student Test Data and English Language Learners With/Without Disabilities

- ◆ Do you have a list of your ELL students with/without disabilities?
- ◆ Do you know if your assessment practices are accessible to all?

Why Is This Important?

Disaggregating student assessment data for this subset of the population will help to identify targets for instruction as well as areas of strength. The information gathered can help determine how students are progressing, the success of teaching methods in use, and areas where additional support might be needed in accommodating the cultural and linguistic needs of students. Failing to put measures in place could affect your ability to "create a culture of assessment literacy … to improve student learning and program effectiveness" for your ELL students with and without disabilities (Lazarus et al., 2022, p. 86).

Collaborate with your director of special education, ENL teacher, and other representatives (e.g., directors of technology and curriculum and instruction, pupil personnel, speech therapist) to determine what type of training would benefit teachers in working with this population, as well as identifying necessary accommodations and accessibility supports, such as the use of bilingual electronic dictionaries, which may or may not be available with current measures in use (Liu et al., 2022).

Discipline—IDEA vs. State Regulations

◆ To ensure compliance with disciplinary procedures, Part B of IDEA (34 C.F.R. § 300.530) provides in-depth guidance on determining appropriate measures to address students with disabilities who have violated the school's code of conduct.

◆ Refer to your state's specific guidelines to identify any variations. For example, New York State also follows the *Part 201 of the Regulations of the Commissioner of Education: Procedural Safeguards for Students with Disabilities Subject to Discipline*.

Why Is This Important?

IDEA is a federal law that includes guidelines for handling disciplinary matters involving students with disabilities. From a compliance stance, ensure that your decisions and actions align with federal, state, and school board policies, serving as a safeguard against potential legal challenges. However, of fundamental importance is also the need to be cognizant of and address any possible imbalances or disproportionality in disciplinary actions involving students with disabilities. The Civil Rights Data Collection (CRDC) released its latest survey report for the 2020–21 school year. The report brings to light a continuing trend where students with disabilities are being disciplined at higher rates than students without disabilities. Therefore, it is vital to actively notice and rectify any imbalances and disproportionality in how discipline is managed, and be mindful of the process, procedures, and the importance of working collaboratively with your school team to create a safe learning environment that respects and protects the rights and interests of students with disabilities.

NYS Update: The NYS Board of Regents issued regulatory amendments effective August 2023. The changes apply to the manifestation process and what is now termed, "Disciplinary Change in Placement" (DCIP) in the suspension process for students with disabilities. The intent is to move toward a more proactive and responsive approach to discipline. The edits also cover a range of measures such as banning corporal punishment, aversive interventions, prone restraint and seclusion, use of timeout and restraint, and data collection. As a result, school districts must adjust their policy guidelines in these areas and conduct annual staff training sessions that also include crisis-intervention tactics and de-escalation methods. Due to the new regulations, it is essential to collaborate with your director of special education and administrative team to ensure proper understanding of the revised disciplinary interventions, now replaced with proactive and restorative practices.

Box 2.2 Discipline Updates

In light of the changes in school disciplinary regulations in New York State, refer to your state's guidelines and school policies for any revisions.

Home Instruction

Whether or not you are responsible for overseeing the home instruction of students for reasons like illness, injury, or personal circumstances, keep the following in mind to ensure that students with IEPs or 504 plans continue to progress in their academic programs:

- ◆ Is there a written process in place?
- ◆ Who is responsible for notifying the teacher that their student is on home instruction?
- ◆ What is the physician's documented date of return to school?
- ◆ Who is gathering the classwork for the student?

♦ Is the home instruction provider aware of the student's individual academic needs, specific concerns, IEP, or 504 plan?
♦ Who will be responsible for grading the work—the home instruction teachers or the actual teachers of record?
♦ Are the classes being conducted virtually, or can the student just sign in to their student portal to access their assignments?
♦ Is there a clear channel for exchanging information, assignments, and feedback, which helps students stay engaged and connected to their school community even when physically absent?
♦ Is there a mechanism in place to monitor progress (e.g., periodic assessments, check-ins, virtual meetings to evaluate their understanding of the curriculum and provide feedback on their work)?

Why Is This Important?
Every student of compulsory school age has the right to receive home instruction. Having a defined plan encourages inclusivity by ensuring that all students can access their education equally, taking into account their needs and emphasizing the importance of maintaining continuous learning. Obtain a list identifying which teachers are available for home instruction, the grades/subjects they teach and how long they can provide instruction for. Refer to the teacher contract for information regarding a stipend for home instruction.

Communities of Student Care and Support

School Nurse Responsibility
♦ Confirm that the school nurse has arranged informative meetings for respective faculty and staff members about specific healthcare needs of identified students that require additional attention. Invite the parents/guardians of these students to the meetings as well to provide clarifying information and foster meaningful communication and relationships.

Why Is This Important?

These meetings are an essential step in promoting a safe and supportive environment for students with both IEPs and 504 plans.

The following is a suggested outline to ensure the success of these meetings:

- ◆ Secure a date, time, and place for the meetings. Invite the relevant faculty and staff (school physician where necessary), as well as parents/guardians. Emphasize how important their participation and assistance are.
- ◆ Check that the schedule doesn't conflict with school events.
- ◆ Prepare an agenda that lists the topics to be covered, like health requirements (e.g., severe allergies, chronic illnesses, medication procedures), emergency plans, communication guidelines, and general health updates.
- ◆ Let the school nurse lead the meetings since they are knowledgeable about healthcare needs.
- ◆ Have any necessary materials available for reference (e.g., informational brochures).
- ◆ If there have been similar situations that the school has handled in the past, mention how well they were handled.
- ◆ Keep detailed meeting records that include who was in attendance, and any action points or follow-up items discussed. These records are critical in case of potential issues.
- ◆ Maintain communication throughout the school year to address any new developments or concerns regarding students' health needs.

Professional Community for Teachers and Staff

Case Managers

- ◆ Ask your director of special education to provide a list of special education teachers, pupil personnel, and related services providers who will be the point of contact for your students with IEPs (some schools also include students with 504 plans as well as those placed out of district as per CSE recommendations).

Why Is This Important?

The case manager is generally the primary point of contact for questions relating to students' IEP programs and participates in the CSE meetings of students on their respective caseloads. This person serves as a critical connection for you if any concerns come to your attention from parents, faculty, staff, or possibly an outside agency representative such as Child Protective Services.

How case managers are chosen can vary. The director of special education can assign them or wait for special education providers to meet (possibly during a Superintendent's Conference Day before the start of school) to determine their own student lists as some individuals may have developed productive, trusting, preexisting relationships with students, siblings, and parents, which contributes to positive family-school partnerships. Depending on your school's process, case managers can also be assigned to your students in out-of-district day placements and residential programs. Having information on students in these settings will be helpful should considerations be given to them returning to the district, participating in school activities, etc.

Meaningful Engagement of Families and Community

Home-School Communication for Non-English-Speaking Parents/Guardians

♦ Is the director of technology aware that schools are required to take reasonable steps to furnish parents with information in a language they can comprehend? Notices placed on the website should be accessible in a language other than English (LOTE) to enable parents/guardians the opportunity to be informed.

Why Is This Important?

Schools are to make efforts toward offering information in a language other than English (LOTE) as mandated by Title VI of the Civil Rights Act of 1964 (42 U.S.C. § 2000[d]). Establishing and maintaining effective communication channels is essential as you work toward fostering a more inclusive and participatory environment for native-language families in your school community.

This can be accomplished in multiple ways:

1. Have the ability to translate documents, like CPSE/CSE paperwork, disciplinary letters, newsletters, and school policies, into their native language.
2. Advertise workshops that provide academic assistance, parenting support, and English instruction.
3. Note where support is available to help families access resources and explore educational options.
4. List opportunities for families to get involved by volunteering at events or participating in classroom activities.

Operations and Management

Integrated Co-Teacher Planning Time

◆ Arrange a time for special education and general education co-teachers to meet before September and begin planning for the school year to discuss students' goals and objectives, accommodations, progress monitoring, etc.

◆ If teacher aides/assistants are assigned to these classes, have them attend the meetings where appropriate.

◆ Review the master schedule to ensure that co-planning periods are incorporated.

Why Is This Important?

Multiple factors contribute to a successful co-teaching program: the type of model being used, expectations, how well teachers are able to communicate effectively with each other, align curricular delivery and materials, and clarify respective responsibilities. Proactive planning before the school year helps establish a foundation for collaborative partnerships that benefit the students.

Finding time for co-planning meetings during the school day can be challenging, but consider the following as possible options:

◆ Depending on the school schedule, some districts are able to use the first 30–40 minutes of the day as "non-contact student time" before buses arrive, which allows for a variety of meetings (e.g., co-teacher, faculty, grade-level, professional learning communities, etc.).

◆ Explore how special area subjects, such as art, music, or physical education can be scheduled to enable grade-level teachers to meet simultaneously.

◆ Incorporate two-hour delays (even if only at the start of each quarter marking period) to plan for the following 10 weeks. This isn't the best option … but it's a possibility.

Review Class Lists

◆ Take a fresh look at your class lists and review enrollment numbers. Identify any changes in sections that have adult support from teacher aides/assistants as well as revisions to their specific assignments (e.g., 1:1 support for specific subjects, travel between classes, etc.).

◆ Request an updated list of your students with IEPs and 504 plans and review it against your class lists to check for accuracy; forward any corrections/concerns that need to be addressed to the office of special education.

Why Is This Important?

A principal can count on three things at this juncture: new entrants (with or without IEPs or 504 plans), students recently classified over the summer, and class adjustments. Whether these are revisions to teaching assignments, integrated co-teaching sections, student assignments per aide/assistant, or room placements, maintaining class lists is a juggling act.

Sometimes there is a disconnect between lists based on entry errors or in time frames between completed meetings and when IEPs or 504 plans are finalized in the system. Staying current will inform you of any further needs, such as arranging professional development, hiring additional personnel, making program changes, or room facilitation adjustments.

Student Management System—IEP/504 Access and Communication Log

◆ Confirm that your current students with IEPs and 504 plans are uploaded and accessible in your SMS (e.g., Infinite Campus; PowerSchool; Frontline; e-School). Some districts have an automatic connection through their SMS, while others may not, so best to double-check.

Why Is This Important?

According to federal regulations (34 C.F.R. § 300.323[d]), teachers and related service staff are required to have access to students' IEPs; 504 plans should also populate. Since faculty will be arriving later this month to prepare their rooms for the upcoming school year, it is important to have all student information uploaded so they can effectively plan and collaborate with colleagues before students arrive on the first day.

If your district has scheduled Superintendent Conference Days for this month or early September, inform your faculty to use the SMS to maintain a comprehensive log of parent phone calls and conferences, verbal communication, resolutions, and follow-ups. In situations where questions may arise during CSE meetings, particularly by a parent advocate or attorney, about instances of parent/guardian contact, this log serves as *vital* evidence of such. Verbal communication without documented evidence *will not* suffice. In essence, effective communication (and progress monitoring) *cannot* be substantiated if it is not supported by written documentation.

Bus Driver/Bus Monitor Training

◆ Ask your director of special education if any bus driver and/or bus monitor training has been scheduled prior to the start of the year. Note if your school district owns the buses or contracts out for busing (the latter so you have a point of contact).

Why Is This Important?

The safe transport of students to and from school is an enormous responsibility and liability. Providing training for bus drivers and bus monitors in areas pertaining to student transportation, particularly those with special needs, is highly advantageous. There are often specific concerns such as special seating for students or a bus plan that your drivers should be aware of on a "need-to-know" basis so they can manage any related issues accordingly. Workshops could encompass various topics such as empathy training, disability awareness, de-escalation techniques, and specific necessities for students who require wheelchair transport or medical assistance. Discuss said trainings with the directors of transportation and special education.

Section 504

◆ Have you been appointed the Section 504 Coordinator for your building?

◆ If not, do you know who is?

◆ Are you aware of the distinctions between 504 and IDEA?

Why Is This Important?

Whether you are the assigned coordinator or not, having knowledge of Section 504 of the Rehabilitation Act of 1973 is of tremendous importance when securing support for students. Section 504 is a civil rights law under the jurisdiction of the Office of Civil Rights (OCR), vs. IDEA, which is a federal law monitored by the Office of Special Education Programs (OSEP).

It is designed to prevent discrimination, protect the civil rights of a student with a handicapping condition as defined in the regulation, and ensure their ability to access their educational program.

In short, Section 504 defines a handicapped person as one who "has a physical or mental impairment which substantially limits one or more major activities, has a record of such an impairment, or is regarded as having such an impairment" (34 C.F.R. § 104.3[J][1][i]-[iii]).

If a student meets the criteria for a 504 plan, they are eligible to receive accommodations and modifications according to their

TABLE 2.1 Key Subparts of Section 504

34 CFR §§ 104.1–104.10	Subpart A—General Provisions
34 CFR §§ 104.31–104.39	Subpart D—Preschool, Elementary, and Secondary Education
34 CFR §§ 104.41–104.47	Subpart E—Postsecondary Education

Source: Wright & Wright (2023)

specific needs. For example, a student may suffer from severe migraines and require accommodations such as extended time for tests and assignments or quiet space to rest. A 504 plan is *not* an IEP, which indicates that a student has a disability requiring special education services in order for them to access their educational program.

Understanding the criteria is important for applying this regulation appropriately since there are distinct variations in eligibility requirements between Section 504 and IDEA; therefore, attending a training is essential. If you are unable to attend a training in time for the start of school, a recommendation is to ask your director of special education to speak at a faculty meeting in September to discuss the distinctions between the two, offer clarification, and respond to any questions they may have. This will provide the necessary information about which direction to pursue should they choose to seek either pathway for student support.

Individuals with Disabilities Education Act

◆ Does the IDEA encompass *all* you need to know about special education protocols for students with disabilities?

◆ Do you know the key areas of emphasis for you in the law?

Why Is This Important?

The Individuals with Disabilities Act 2004 (IDEA) is federal legislation that guarantees children between the ages of 3–21 who have been diagnosed with a disability the right to a free appropriate public education, commonly known as FAPE. Moreover, all special education and related services are to be tailored to address the student's needs and equip them for further education, employment, and independent living opportunities (20 U.S.C. § 1400 et seq.)

To qualify for dedicated special education funding, each state must create its own set of special statutes and regulations that align with IDEA (2004). For example, New York State also follows the *Part 200 of the Regulations of the Commissioner of Education: Students with Disabilities*. While states have the authority to establish standards that exceed federal law, they cannot reduce the rights already guaranteed by it. For example, a state can change the qualifying criteria for "Other Health Impairment" but still have to maintain the 13 disability categories listed under IDEA, however, it is not uncommon for states to offer more entitlements than what is already outlined in the law. Therefore, it is important to know the distinctions between your state's regulations and federal language. This will help ensure legal compliance in interpreting and managing special education as a school leader.

Box 2.3 Part 200 NYS Example

Example: As a principal in New York State under *Part 200 of the NYS Regulations of the Commissioner of Education for Students with Disabilities*, you are entitled to receive notice of an initial CSE referral filed on behalf of one of your students. You have ten days from the date of the referral to meet with the parent/guardian to discuss if the student would benefit from general education support services as an alternative to pursuing a special education referral (8 C.R.R.-NY § 200.4[a][4][5][9][i]-[iii]).

TABLE 2.2 Key Sections of IDEA

20 U.S.C. §1400	Findings and Purposes of IDEA
20 U.S.C. §1401	Definitions
20 U.S.C. §1412	State Eligibility—Child Find, LRE, Tuition Reimbursement
20 U.S.C. §1414 (a–d)	Evaluations, Eligibility, IEPs
20 U.S.C. §1415	Procedural Safeguards—IEE, PWN, Due Process, Court, Discipline, Exhaustion

Source: Wright & Wright (2023)

School Improvement

State Performance Plan for Federal Indicators

◆ The purpose of the plan is to assess each state's implementation of IDEA under defined areas called indicators. The 17 indicators focus on either compliance or student results. OSEP sets the targets for identified compliance indicators, and each state sets its own measurable targets for the results indicators.

Why Is This Important?

Under IDEA, each state is required to develop a state performance plan and yearly report that evaluates their efforts toward both implementing and meeting the intent of the IDEA. The state performance plan indicators provide clear goals for you to work toward.

Examples of results indicators are Graduation Rates, Dropout Rates, Suspension/Expulsion, Parent Involvement, and LRE-School Age.

Sample compliance indicators are Suspension/Expulsion by Race/Ethnicity, Disproportionality in Special Education by Race/Ethnicity, Child Find and Secondary Transition.

The data obtained can help identify areas that require improvement and assist in making well-informed decisions to enhance outcomes for your students with disabilities. The director of special education has the necessary information and can provide details about the specific indicator being monitored for your district in the upcoming year.

August Checklist

Did you …

- [ ] arrange a committee to disaggregate your assessment data for ELL students with/without disabilities, identify strengths and challenges in test performance, and identify any professional development needed to address language accessibility issues (e.g., teaching specific academic vocabulary)?
- [ ] review your district's policies and practices regarding the discipline of students with disabilities?
- [ ] confirm if a home instruction plan is in place, and do you oversee it?
- [ ] check in with the school nurse about scheduling any necessary meetings to prepare for students who have significant health/medical challenges as noted on their IEP?
- [ ] contact the director of special education for a case manager list and an updated teacher aide/assistant assignment list, inquire if bus driver/bus monitor training is being scheduled, confirm that CSE documentation is sent home in a language other than English as applicable (e.g., disciplinary letters) and ask what the performance indicator is for this year?
- [ ] ask your director of technology if IEPs and 504 plans are accessible in the SMS, and if information on the school website is accessible in a language other than English?
- [ ] compare IDEA with your state's special education regulations?

References

Civil Rights Act of 1964, 42 U.S.C. § 2000d. (1964). https://www.law.cornell.edu/uscode/text/42/2000d

Elementary and Secondary Education Act, 20 U.S.C. 6825 § 3115 (2024). https://uscode.house.gov/view.xhtml?req=granuleid:USC-prelim-title20-section6825&num=0&edition=prelim

Elementary and Secondary Education Act, 20 U.S.C. 6312 § 1112 (2016). https://www2.ed.gov/documents/essa-act-of-1965.pdf

IDEA Regulations, 34 C.F.R. § 300.530 (2017). https://sites.ed.gov/idea/regs/b/e/300.530

IDEA Regulations, 34 C.F.R. § 300.323 (2017). https://sites.ed.gov/idea/regs/b/d/300.323/d

Individuals with Disabilities Education Act of 2004, 20 U.S.C. § 1400 et seq. (2010). https://www.law.cornell.edu/uscode/text/20/1400

Lazarus, S.S., Brookhart, S. M., Ghere, G. & Liu, K. (2022). Improving local assessment practices for students with disabilities. *Journal of Special Education*, 35(2), 86–98.

Liu, K., Thurlow, M., & Peterson, D. H. (2022). Including English learners with disabilities in assessments. *Journal of Special Education*, 35(2), 99–111.

State of New York. Commissioner of Education. (2024). *Part 200 of the Regulations of the Commissioner.* New York State Education Department. https://www.nysed.gov/special-education/section-2004-procedures-referral-evaluation-iep-development-placement-and-review

State of New York. Commissioner of Education. (2024). *Part 201 of the Regulations of the Commissioner.* New York State Education Department. https://www.nysed.gov/special-education/part-201-regulations-commissioner

Section 504 of the Rehabilitation Act of 1973, 34 C.F.R. § 104.3 (n.d.). https://www2.ed.gov/policy/rights/reg/ocr/edlite-34cfr104.html#S3

U. S. Department of Education, Office for Civil Rights. (2023). *2020-21 Civil Rights Data Collection.* https://www2.ed.gov/about/offices/list/ocr/docs/crdc-educational-opportunities-report.pdf

Wright, P. W. D., & Wright, P. D. (2023). *Special education law* (3rd ed.). Harbor House Law Press.

Part II
First Quarter Marking Period

3

September

The following principal leadership standards support your tasks for this month.

Box 3.1 PSEL 2015 and Promoting Principal Leadership for the Success of Students with Disabilities

Effective principals …

(2) adhere to professional norms; possess an ethical mindset; and promote said behaviors among faculty and staff in supporting students with disabilities.

(4) communicate high academic expectations for students with disabilities; develop teacher capacity for effective instruction; implement valid monitoring and assessment systems; ensure evidence-based, differentiated approaches to instruction, and implement technology for teaching and learning.

(5) build a safe, caring, and healthy environment for students with disabilities that promotes inclusivity and opportunities to learn from their non-disabled peers to the greatest extent possible and encourages them to be active, responsible members of their community.

DOI: 10.4324/9781003483045-5

(6) evaluate teaching practice that supports improving and achieving outcomes for students with disabilities.

(7) establish a sense of collective responsibility and mutual accountability for the success of students with disabilities.

(8) create partnerships with families through public and private sectors to support student learning in and out of school.

(9) manage school structures, operations, and systems to support students with disabilities.

(10) know, comply with, and help the school community understand local, state, and federal laws, rights, policies, and regulations so as to promote student success.

Ethics and Professional Norms

Confidentiality of IEPs and 504 Plans

◆ Emphasize to faculty and staff the critical importance of preserving the privacy of student-specific information when discussing IEPs or 504 plans.

Why Is This Important?

Protecting the privacy of student data is not just an obligation but a legal necessity as outlined in IDEA (34 C.F.R. § 300.610). This includes safeguarding information and all details related to records, assessments, and services. IDEA also reinforces the guidelines set forth in the Family Educational Rights and Privacy Act (FERPA) (20 U.S.C. § 1232[g][a][4][A]) concerning what constitutes "educational records" in connection with school-maintained student files.

Conversations happen, whether in the cafeteria, faculty room, at school sports events, or in parking lots, supermarkets, and homes. Caution faculty and staff on inadvertent disclosure of sensitive information, especially in smaller districts where one is not always aware of staff or substitutes who may know of individuals or be related.

Curriculum, Instruction, and Assessment

Local Student Assessments

Send a reminder to your teachers to review the schedule for administering computer-based local assessments such as STAR or i-Ready, and to arrange any accommodations for students with IEPs or 504 plans in their class.

Why Is This Important?

Implementing this additional step will ensure that students have the necessary access to assessments to demonstrate their skills in the areas being evaluated, both for progress monitoring and compliance reasons.

Communities of Student Care and Support

Assistive Technology—School Website and LOTE

◆ Follow up with your director of technology regarding the posting of school events (e.g., open house, sports, clubs, enrichment opportunities, etc.) on the school website and availability in LOTE for student access.

Why Is This Important?

Students who are enrolled in out-of-district day programs recommended by the CSE, such as BOCES in New York State, are not physically present in the school building and, as a result, might not have direct knowledge of extracurricular activities or school events. However, they are entitled to participate in these opportunities. By making this information available in LOTE, they have the means to be informed and involved.

Professional Capacity of School Personnel

Special Education Teacher Evaluations

◆ Review your list of special education teachers and note their respective assignments, whether they work in integrated co-teaching settings, resource rooms, or special classes, serve in a direct/indirect consultant teacher capacity, or travel between multiple schools as itinerant teachers.

◆ Before proceeding with formal evaluations, take time to visit those specific classrooms to identify distinctive features of their classroom setup, teaching methodologies, materials utilized, speak with the students, etc.

Why Is This Important?

"Special education teachers work under a variety of complex conditions, with a very heterogeneous population, and support student progress through a very individualized set of goals" (Johnson & Semmelroth, 2014, p. 71); hence the importance of pre-observations (as well as walk-throughs) cannot be overstated. They are incredibly informative in understanding class dynamics and beneficial to the quality of feedback provided. As the evaluator, you are in the position of processing the variety of approaches special educators adopt to address the complex learning needs of their students (e.g., specially designed instruction vs. differentiation). During the pre-observation meeting, you can ask to see where students' IEP goals will be incorporated into the lesson vs. just looking to see what course content is being covered during the observation. Frequent visits also present the opportunity to identify curricular alignment between your general and special education teachers. Is "instruction … intellectually challenging and authentic to student experiences and educational objectives, responsive to student strengths, evidence-based, and differentiated?" (Council of Chief State School Officers, 2017, p. 7) or does a silo mentality prevail, which counteracts your mission to create a shared understanding of the importance of "collaboration, community, and inclusivity" (Council of Chief State School Officers, 2017, p. 3). The time spent observing and speaking with your teachers is time well-spent, given that in the final analysis, the focus is on the improvement of instructional practices for the benefit of all students.

Professional Community for Teachers and Staff

Cohort Meetings for Student Monitoring

◆ Consider scheduling quarterly (or trimester) cohort meetings with your guidance counselors, social worker, school psychologist, assistant principal, and director of special education to review changes to grade-level rosters, confirm cohort placement, and discuss students with IEPs who may be at risk of not graduating, advancing to the next grade level, or passing the marking period.

Why Is This Important?

By participating in this process, individuals can address any concerns that might be impeding students from achieving academic success and propose necessary follow-up actions such as the addition of academic intervention, accessing social services for student or family support, consideration of CSE program reviews, assigning a mentor, and more. It also draws attention to grade levels with a higher proportion of classified students, prompting further analysis. For high school students, it identifies those who may be in between grade levels based on credits earned, which may impact course scheduling for next year. In schools with frequent student turnover, the meetings help monitor students' educational progress and need for additional support given their history of varied school placements.

Case Manager Follow-Up

◆ Confirm that teachers are not only informed about who the case managers are for students in their class, but that they are also aware of the content of their IEP or 504 plans and related responsibilities.

Why Is This Important?

Ensuring that teachers are informed of the content of students' IEPs and 504 plans is essential on many fronts; compliance is one. Documentation supports their awareness of and responsibilities for implementation. Case managers should be communicating with the providers so they know who to contact if there are student concerns during the year. You want to avoid situations where, during a CSE meeting, a teacher indicates in the presence of a parent and possibly an advocate, that they were unaware the student had an IEP or 504 plan. Once that is said, the lack of provision of FAPE becomes a significant compliance issue.

Meaningful Engagement of Families and Community

Child Find Responsibilities

◆ Review your district's policies and procedures regarding Child Find obligations under IDEA.

Why Is This Important?

As mandated by IDEA, under Child Find, schools have a responsibility to seek out, locate, and evaluate any child suspected of having a disability and requiring special education. Included are children who are homeschooled, migrants, homeless, wards of the state, in private schools or even advancing from grade to grade (34 C.F.R. § 300.111[a]-[d]). As a result, schools must allocate funds for community outreach efforts. This could involve distributing brochures through the mail or making them available at all district schools and main offices, placing ads, sharing information on the district's website, discussing at the board of education (BOE) meetings or at parent–teacher association (PTA) meetings, engaging in conversations with daycare providers or private school staff members. This highlights the significance of allocating monies in the budget the prior school year to carry out said activities. To ensure coordination, contact your director of special education to collaborate on a process for managing the requirements.

Operations and Management

Transfer Students with an IEP or 504 Plan

◆ Inform your secretary to notify you when transfer students arrive with IEPs or 504 plans from other districts. This information is necessary for assessing any potential impact on staffing and class sections.

◆ Review your current enrollments to identify sections that are capped and which classes have adult supports (teacher aides/assistants, possibly direct/indirect consultant teachers).

Why Is This Important?

Regularly checking your class lists is vital for monitoring enrollment and determining whether adjustments may be needed such as reassigning staff, creating a new class section, or possibly the need for new hires. This practice is particularly important when accommodating transfer students who require a range of resources or supports outlined in their IEP, bearing in mind that the receiving school is to honor the transfer IEP pending a CSE meeting. Based on experience, a transfer student is generally reviewed by the CSE within 30 days of entry and a new IEP is in effect within 60 days of arrival (8 C.R.R.-NY § 200.4[b]). The 504 plans of transfer students are also reviewed, however, there is no regulation stipulating a timeframe. A recommendation would be to stay with a similar time frame as a student with an IEP so they receive an updated plan to meet their needs in a new setting.

State Assessment Preparation

◆ Stay current on your test ordering and administration schedule for the school year.

Why Is This Important?

When ordering exams, obtain a current list of accommodations from the office of special education and inquire about any training provided for exam proctoring and administering of test accommodations. Identify if specific formats, such as enlarged print, are necessary. If computer-based tests are being given, they may already include accommodations like calculators or read-aloud texts. Additionally, note if scribes or readers will be needed for paper-based exams. Some districts may have the director of special education or CSE chairperson automatically forward information on specific test formats to be ordered, others may not; best to be prepared

McKinney–Vento Homeless Assistance Act

◆ Students eligible under the McKinney–Vento Act are those without a stable, consistent, and sufficient nighttime residence (42 U.S.C. § 11434a[2][A][B][i]-[iv]) and who require specific supports for them to participate fully in educational programs at school. This may include students living in shared accommodations, a trailer park, or their vehicles or are unaccompanied youth who meet the housing criteria. Inquire if any of your students with disabilities or 504 plans fall under this category.

Why Is This Important?

Educating your school faculty and staff will increase awareness and provide a means for addressing any concerns brought to their attention. Title 1 Part A funds are available through the Every Student Succeeds Act (ESSA) to assist students who meet the criteria. For details, contact your director of special education, who usually oversees McKinney–Vento, and is responsible for ensuring students receive the necessary support and assistance to succeed academically via collaboration and interagency coordination (unless your district has assigned another individual who specifically manages this). Additionally, data concerning your school's homeless student population is typically included in your state's school report card, further highlighting the importance of early identification and assistance in supporting these students effectively.

September Checklist

Did you …

- [ ] reinforce to your faculty and staff the importance of maintaining IEP confidentiality at all times?
- [ ] confirm with your teachers their awareness of student accommodations for local progress monitoring assessments and to follow up on any concerns?
- [ ] verify with your director of technology that all school-related extracurricular activities, events, clubs, etc., are accessible on the district's website and in LOTE?
- [ ] schedule a time to visit your special education classrooms?
- [ ] schedule quarterly (or trimester) cohort meetings for student monitoring purposes?
- [ ] check on the process for informing faculty of students' IEPs and 504 plans?
- [ ] obtain a list of case managers for your identified students?
- [ ] confer with your director of special education regarding Child Find requirements?
- [ ] follow up on transfer students with IEPs or 504 plans and assess status of class enrollments and associated support staff?
- [ ] request a current list of accommodations to ensure the correct ordering of state test exams?
- [ ] address McKinney–Vento with your staff and speak with the requisite liaison regarding supplemental services available under Title 1 funding?

References

Council of Chief State School Officers. (2017). *PSEL 2015 and promoting principal leadership for the success of students with disabilities.* https://www.ccsso.org/sites/default/files/2017-10/PSELforSWDs01252017_0.pdf

Family Educational Rights and Privacy Act of 1974, 20 U.S.C. § 1232g (2013). https://www.law.cornell.edu/uscode/text/20/1232g#a_4

IDEA Regulations, 34 C.F.R. § 300.111 (2017). https://sites.ed.gov/idea/regs/b/b/300.111

IDEA Regulations, 34 C.F.R. § 300.610 (2024). https://www.ecfr.gov/current/title-34/subtitle-B/chapter-III/part-300/subpart-F/subject-group-ECFR1d2a18271819883/section-300.610

Johnson, E. & Semmelroth, C.L. (2014). Special education teacher evaluation: Why it matters, what makes it challenging, and how to address these challenges. *Assessment for Effective Intervention*, 39(2), 71–82. https://doi.org/10.117/1534508413513315

McKinney-Vento Homeless Assistance Act of 1987, 42 U.S.C. § 11434a (2024). https://codes.findlaw.com/us/title-42-the-public-health-and-welfare/42-usc-sect-11434a/

State of New York. Commissioner of Education. (2023). *Part 200 of the Regulations of the Commissioner.* New York State Education Department. https://www.nysed.gov/special-education/section-2004-procedures-referral-evaluation-iep-development-placement-and-review

4

October

The following principal leadership standards support your tasks for this month.

Box 4.1 PSEL 2015 and Promoting Principal Leadership for the Success of Students with Disabilities

Effective principals …

(3) communicate high academic expectations for students with disabilities; use multi-tiered systems of support; implement valid monitoring and assessment systems; ensure evidence-based, differentiated approaches to instruction; and implement technology for teaching and learning.

(9) manage school structures, operations, and systems to support students with disabilities.

(10) establish an imperative for improvement by emphasizing the "why" and "how" of change.

Curriculum, Instruction, and Assessment

Five-Week Progress Reports
♦ Concerns about a classified student's academic performance may be expressed at this early date.

DOI: 10.4324/9781003483045-6

Why Is This Important?

A teacher may express concerns about a student's academic standing as a result of local testing and classroom performance, which might warrant consideration for additional support or continued progress monitoring. A referral to the Child Study Team (CST), which may also be known as the Instructional Support Team (IST) or another term in your school, can be submitted as long as the reasons for the meeting *will not* impact the student's IEP. For example, if the intent is to discuss the application of building-level AIS for additional math or reading support, that is appropriate.

Concerns that necessitate amending the IEP would require a CSE program review. Note that not every state uses the CSE term as Texas refers to its committee as Admissions Review Dismissal (ARD), so check the specific terminology applied in your state.

There is a form that allows for changes to an IEP with parental consent and a sign-off by the CSE representative. It may be called "Proposed Amendment to IEP Form Without a Committee Meeting" or "Request to Consent to Amend an IEP Without a Meeting" or a similar title. It is not used for programmatic changes to the IEP, generally for adjustments to accommodations and modifications, however, consult the director of special education for specifics.

Monitor Assistive Technology

◆ Continue to stay abreast of any additional assistive technology needs or access concerns.

Why Is This Important?

Assistive technology tools for students may have been upgraded, modified, or sent out for repair with no replacement on hand (e.g., an FM system for a student who is hard of hearing). Inform your teachers and/or case managers to keep you apprised of any necessary changes so adjustments enabling students continued instructional access can be made; the director of special education is to be informed as well. Additionally, you may want to consider requesting an updated assistive technology list from the office of special education every quarter (or trimester) to review the types of equipment your students are using, such as adapted desks (e.g., standing desks). Speak with related service providers if you have any questions regarding assistive tools being used by students on their caseload. Keep in mind that equipment or furniture will need to be stored for students at the end of the year. Having an idea of what is in use will enable you to determine a dedicated storage area come June unless the equipment is being turned in to the office of special education.

Operations and Management

Transfer Students with an IEP or 504 Plan

◆ Continue to monitor class enrollment numbers in preparation for transfer students with IEPs or 504 plans. Sometimes there is a sudden influx in the beginning of the year and then it levels off.

Why Is This Important?

You want to avoid the need for sudden class adjustments; staying current on your numbers gives you a "heads up." Also, keep in mind that reallocating a teacher aide or assistant from a student's program, as specified in their IEP, for another assignment, like covering a different class as new entrants have now exceeded the class size limit stipulated in board policy, violates the student's IEP and their right to FAPE. It is best to mitigate adverse effects from this action by having a contingency strategy in place and staying current on your enrollment numbers and class sections.

Classroom Student Groupings and Service Provision

◆ Be cognizant of how many classified, 504, and ELL students are grouped in a general education classroom (including integrated co-teaching).

Why Is This Important?

Allocating multiple service providers to one or more classrooms appears beneficial from a remedial stance. However, this approach *may* not be the best fit due to each student's distinct needs, the number of related services providers "in play" at any given time, and the provision of push-in, pull-out, and direct consultant teacher support. Some providers may also be itinerant and have fixed times that they can be in the building on any given day. It's worth keeping an eye on as sometimes too many providers in/out of a classroom can be disruptive. And taking a student/s out of their classroom for instruction in a hallway doesn't meet the intent of their IEP if services are to be delivered *in* a co-teaching class.

School Improvement

NYS Verification Reports

- ◆ The information required to complete the NYS Verification Reports (VR) is imported from the Student Information Repository System (SIRS) and accessible online in October to the director of special education.
- ◆ It applies to students ages 4–5 or 6–21 who are receiving special education services.
- ◆ Though these particular reports are specific to NYS, the information may be available under different headings in your state because of how special education is monitored.
- ◆ The reports are critical for maintaining accurate data and ensuring compliance with regulations.

Why Is This Important?

The reports offer valuable insights into your student population, including demographic information, disability distribution, and placement in the least restrictive environment. By analyzing this data, both educators and administrators can make informed decisions to enhance educational outcomes and create a more inclusive environment for all students. Note that if the data highlights potential issues, the district will be alerted and may need to follow a required monitoring process.

NYS Verification Report 2—School Age Child Count by Age and Disability

- ◆ An analysis of the data might indicate a higher percentage of students with a specific disability in 4th grade (given the age), which could prompt further review of curricular and instructional practices.

NYS Verification Report 3—School Age Students by Disability and Race/Ethnicity

♦ The purpose of the VR-3 is to examine student classifications for any disparities.

NYS Verification Report 5—School Age Least Restrictive Environment Setting

♦ How many of your students are being educated in the least restrictive environment in varied settings (e.g., special class, general education, residential, parentally placed in a nonpublic school, incarcerated in county correctional facilities, etc.)? In what age range? By what percentage? (80% or more? Less than 79% of the time? Less than 40%?) And what is their disability? How many of these students can be scheduled for increased time in district and/or in the least restrictive environment?

NYS Verification Report 8—District Report of School-Age Students By Building of Enrollment

♦ Do you know where your students are? The VR-8 identifies the setting where your students are being educated.

October Checklist

Did you …

- ☐ address any five-week progress report concerns expressed by your teachers about their students with IEPs at this point in the year?
- ☐ follow up on any assistive technology needs regarding equipment or access?
- ☐ review your class enrollments and associated support staff availability?
- ☐ identify if you have too many providers attached to a class for service provision and adjust accordingly (if possible)?
- ☐ convene a meeting among relevant staff to examine and address any concerns identified in the NYS Verification Reports (or similar reports in your state)?

5

November

The following principal leadership standards support your tasks for this month.

Box 5.1 PSEL 2015 and Promoting Principal Leadership for the Success of Students with Disabilities

Effective principals ...

(4) communicate high academic expectations for students with disabilities; use multi-tiered systems of support, implement valid monitoring and assessment systems; ensure evidence-based, differentiated approaches to instruction; and implement technology for teaching and learning.

(9) manage school structures, operations, and systems to support students with disabilities.

Curriculum, Instruction, and Assessment

Report Cards—End of 1st Quarter

♦ Should an initial CSE referral be considered for a student at this time?

DOI: 10.4324/9781003483045-7

Why Is This Important?

The first report card marking period can be a time when teachers contemplate a CSE referral to *rule out the possibility of a learning disability*, however, this may be premature at this point. A vital question you should ask your teachers to contemplate is whether they have *fully* implemented *all* levels of tiered remedial supports *and* gathered *sufficient* progress monitoring data. IDEA stipulates the implementation of RTI/MTSS and the use of scientific, research-based interventions *prior to* consideration of a Specific Learning Disability (SLD) (20 U.S.C. § 1414[b][6][B]), hence, the importance of how prominent a role your AIS, RTI, and MTSS programs play in the CSE referral process.

Though well-intentioned, remind your faculty that a CSE referral suggests that the student's current difficulties may be attributed to a *disability* impeding success in their current program. Without the inclusion of the aforementioned supports in addition to sufficient progress monitoring data, the necessary prereferral documentation is unavailable for review. Implementing the required proactive measures *prior to* coming to the CSE table is integral to making informed decisions.

Progress Monitoring

- ◆ Do you know what methods your teachers use to progress monitor their students?
- ◆ How is this occurring in your building-level academic support programs?

Why Is This Important?

Accurate progress monitoring provides for informed, quantifiable decision-making to allow for curricular adjustments and targeted interventions. Regular analysis also supports the early identification of at-risk students and the timely implementation of necessary support measures. Ensuring that this is a consistent part of your educational process can significantly contribute to the overall success and responsiveness of your instructional programs. It is a critical aspect when determining how your students with disabilities are progressing toward meeting their goals and objectives or when it is necessary to pursue an initial CSE referral.

Operations and Management

Class Lists and Support Staff Update

◆ Continue to monitor your class enrollment numbers and associated in-class support staff schedules.

Why Is This Important?

Maintaining an awareness of the ratio of special education to general education students in a classroom ensures legal compliance, as does providing the IEP-mandated support staff assistance in the classroom. This ongoing vigilance helps ensure that class sizes remain conducive to effective teaching and learning. If this sounds repetitive, it's because it is. Special education is fluid, so staying informed is essential. When a family with children who have IEPs is sitting in the main office awaiting decisions on a class placement, having a solid grasp of your enrollments and support staff assignments is invaluable. Furthermore, initial CSE meetings, program reviews, and transfer meetings are occurring. Knowing where you have room for student placements and/or the presence of support staff is important.

November Checklist

Did you ...

- ☐ remind your staff of the importance of applying building-level supports prior to consideration of an initial CSE referral?
- ☐ identify the progress monitoring methods being used by teachers and academic intervention providers?
- ☐ update your class enrollments and review the allocation of support staff?

Reference

Individuals with Disabilities Education Act of 2004, 20 USC § 1414 (n.d.). https://law.cornell.edu/uscode/text/20/1414

Part III

Second Quarter Marking Period

6

December

The following principal leadership standards support your tasks for this month.

**Box 6.1 2015 PSEL and Promoting Principal Leadership
for the Success of Students with Disabilities**

Effective principals ...

(4) communicate high academic expectations for students with disabilities; use multi-tiered systems of support; implement valid monitoring and assessment systems; ensure evidence-based, differentiated approaches to instruction; and implement technology for teaching and learning.

(9) assign roles and responsibilities to optimize staff capacity to address each student's learning needs; and manage school structures, operations, and systems to support students with disabilities.

Curriculum, Instruction, and Assessment

Five-Week Progress Reports
- Are the same students experiencing challenges during this reporting period?
- What is the status of interventions applied thus far?

DOI: 10.4324/9781003483045-9

Why Is This Important?

If the student has an IEP, has a CSE program review been held to discuss current concerns paired with data outlining the student's progress toward their IEP goals and objectives thus far? Have accommodations or modifications been amended? Is the student being provided opportunities for additional building-level supports (as students with an IEP are still eligible for AIS, RTI, MTSS)? Has there been ongoing communication with the parents/guardians? Documenting these communications and interventions is key to fostering transparency, ensuring accountability, maintaining an overview of the student's academic progression, and provides insight for future decision-making.

If an initial CSE referral is being considered at this time due to concerns about a possible learning disability, note that questions will still be asked about the extent of RTI/MTSS support to date, the provision of scientific, research-based interventions, frequency of support/s, individual or group instruction, and progress monitoring data.

Operations and Management

Assistive Technology Plan

◆ Is there a specific assistive technology plan in place?

Why Is This Important?

Assistive technology tools can be costly, and there is considerable variety. Listed below are suggestions to discuss with your directors of special education and technology to ensure effective implementation and oversight of tools currently in use or anticipated:

1. **Periodic reviews:** Request an assistive technology list on a quarterly (or trimester) basis from the office of special education to inform you of the specific needs of your students. The case managers can also forward updates. This information will provide insight for budget planning as well.

2. **Professional development:** Offer professional development opportunities for teachers and support staff on specific assistive technology tools currently in use (e.g., speech-to-text software, augmentative communication devices), and other tools to enhance student learning opportunities. Collaborate with your related services providers as they can provide trainings on current tools in use unless a specific vendor is required.

3. **Technology audit:** Review both the physical and digital learning environments to ensure they are fully accessible to students using assistive technology devices.

4. **Planning for testing:** Follow up with your teachers and respective staff to confirm that all necessary assistive technology tools are functional, especially given upcoming local assessment periods (if conducted mid-year in your school) or possibly state testing in January for students graduating early. This not only applies to the tool itself but also ensures that students feel confident using it during testing.

5. **Monitoring and evaluation:** Are surveys conducted to report on the effectiveness of current tools in use both for daily activities and assessments? Input from your students, teachers, related service providers, and parents/guardians can provide invaluable feedback, even if it's just "Works great—student loves using it" or "Student prefers using a regular desk with fidget bands in lieu of the standing desk."

6. **Implementation plan:** The development of a plan would include questions such as, "Who will be using this equipment?" "Is it being purchased or borrowed from a lending library?" "How is it being used in the classroom?" "Does it remain in school or is it used at home as well?" "Who is providing the training and are the parents involved?" and "Who is responsible for repairs?" A determination can be made about what types of equipment a plan such as this would be used for.

7. **Storage:** Is a process in place whereby specific equipment purchased for students is inventoried and labeled for

return at the end of the year? If equipment is also being used at home, is there a form for parent/guardian sign-off and knowledge of responsibility for care?

8. **Budget planning:** With the budget process commencing, advocate for monies that adequately cover the costs of updating, maintaining, and training staff. Financial planning should also anticipate future needs based on student enrollment and an increase in the special education population.

General Annual Review/CSE Meeting Guidance

◆ Do you have adequate room availability so meetings can be held in the same room all day, or do you need to juggle rooms over the course of the day?

◆ Stay informed of the timeline for annual reviews (or other CSE meetings), which will most likely begin in January. However, the start date can vary based on several factors such as the total number of classified students to be reviewed, the availability of CSE chairpersons to lead the meetings, and the allocation of meeting days per week. Your building might be assigned Tuesdays and Thursdays. In addition, some chairpersons may allocate a set number of days per case manager versus different providers over the course of the day. Knowledge of how the meetings will be structured is important so you know how to schedule substitute coverage.

◆ Meeting days and times can change for various reasons (e.g., snow day, parent unavailability, incomplete testing, absence of attendees, etc.), so being updated is important because you have most likely scheduled sub coverage in advance.

◆ Teacher preparation is key to maintaining a focus on the purpose of the meeting and planning for September.

Why Is This Important?

Having a dedicated conference room can indeed optimize the organization and efficiency of CSE meetings held in your building on any given day; however, it is not uncommon to encounter situations where multiple meetings are scheduled simultaneously. Establishing protocols for room reservations (such as outlets for Chromebook or laptop access, need for video conferencing, possibly a projector to convey the IEP, phone access to teleconference, number of participants attending, and space availability for setup) aids in ensuring that meetings run smoothly.

Though notices of upcoming CSE meetings are sent out by the office of special education and specify attendees, parents/guardians might contact you to voice concerns that a particular teacher was not invited. The case manager should communicate with them to manage expectations, as well as inform them that teachers can share their input through written statements. However, if a parent/guardian is of the opinion that the absence of a specific teacher involved in their child's IEP will hinder the development of a new IEP by the CSE committee, they *do* have the right to request another meeting with identified members present.

Remind your faculty that the objective of the annual review meeting is to evaluate a student's progress towards their IEP goals and objectives and make recommendations for September, it is *not* a substitute for a parent-teacher conference. It is necessary to adhere to established times given the planned meetings for the day to avoid disruption to the substitute schedule and prevent teachers from getting their prep or lunch periods, which could prompt a union grievance if you are unable to provide said coverage. No doubt instances happen whereby the meeting goes overtime or is interrupted by a fire drill, but the allotted time is generally sufficient as long as all come prepared with appropriate data and have maintained communication throughout the year. Teachers should be ready to discuss current levels of performance. Comments such as, "Rowan is doing *okay* and is performing *as well as to be expected*" or, "Logan is performing *at about* a year below grade level," will not meet criteria for an accurate, data-based assessment of the student's skills.

Kindergarten Entrants Transitioning from the Committee on Preschool Education

◆ Request a copy of the scheduled meetings for preschoolers who are receiving special education services as a preschool student with a disability (PSD) but "Turning 5" and eligible to enter kindergarten the following September based on your district's guidelines.

Why Is This Important?

Just as in the summer, your kindergarten teacher and possibly some of your related services personnel will most likely be invited to the CSE portion of the meeting. The general meeting process for these students is to begin a discussion of their preschool IEP and determine if summer services (for next year) are indicated. At that point, the meeting shifts to an initial referral under the CSE, all necessary documentation is reviewed, and a determination is made regarding the student's eligibility for classification in one of the 13 disability categories as per the IDEA (34 C.F.R. § 300.8[a]). If eligible, services are recommended for September.

Since December usually signals the start of budget planning, knowledge of these students and their IEP needs will be beneficial as you begin drafting your classes, programs, and staffing needs for September. Additionally, these students are entitled to participate in your kindergarten screening, assuming it is held in the spring. Knowing their names in advance will ensure that parents are notified and their child placed on the schedule.

Substitute Coverage and Annual Review Planning

◆ Do you know where your teacher aides and assistants are?
◆ Do you have sufficient coverage for meetings?
◆ Have you received a CSE meeting schedule?

Why Is This Important?

Navigating the upcoming "annual review season" while ensuring full compliance with students' IEPs or 504 plans requires careful planning and strategic alignment of support staff. Listed below are several strategies that might be helpful:

1. **Plan ahead:** Make sure you know the schedules of your support staff to identify any times when they might be available to cover a teacher's class for a period. Planning ahead can give you the time to address coverage concerns proactively, especially because many schools have a shortage of substitutes. Some districts have contractual language indicating that teachers can only be scheduled for CSE meetings during their prep periods to avoid disrupting instructional time. Inquire if district practice is to allow special education teachers to take an in-school IEP writing day to prepare for annual reviews given the amount of paperwork involved. This additional need for substitute coverage can impact the overall planning, especially if there are already subs in place for CSE meetings on that day. Note that directors of special education may prefer to arrange their own substitute coverage for meetings, so confirm in advance. Maintaining communication will allow for an understanding of building needs and ensure appropriate coverage where needed.

2. **Cross-train your staff:** Consider providing training opportunities for your support staff to enhance flexibility of assignments. This allows individuals to step in for one another when in roles critical for meeting IEP or 504 requirements.

3. **Build a reliable substitute pool:** Having a group of substitute teachers, teacher aides and assistants who are familiar with your school's procedures is a valuable resource. Building this pool before the start of annual reviews would be advantageous.

4. **Prioritize based on need:** Occasions may arise when you have to prioritize student coverage due to staffing shortages. This means that students with the *most urgent* needs as per their IEP will be covered first; not ideal, but a realistic possibility. Keep your director of special education (and 504 coordinator, if needed) informed of any

concerns or specific complaints from parents; transparency is key.

5. **Administrative input:** Seek guidance from your administrative team when substitutes are unavailable and coverage is paramount.

6. **Communication is essential:** Keep your faculty and support staff informed about coverage concerns and potential adjustments and seek their input on handling situations. Collaboration often leads to solutions.

7. **Documentation:** Document staffing decisions affecting IEP or 504 compliance. This is important for explaining circumstances and efforts made to comply if issues arise regarding lack of coverage.

8. **Debrief:** At the conclusion of annual reviews, assess what worked well and where improvements can be made.

December Checklist

Did you …

- [ ] follow up on any student concerns expressed by teachers as a result of the five-week progress reports?
- [ ] touch base with the directors of special education and technology regarding a basic plan for managing assistive technology tools?
- [ ] discuss with your teachers the importance of being prepared for CSE meetings?
- [ ] request a list of preschool students with a disability who are "Turning 5" and eligible to enter kindergarten in September and place their names on the spring kindergarten screening list (if held)?
- [ ] obtain meeting schedules and begin the process of assigning rooms and securing subs?

Reference

IDEA Regulations, 34 C.F.R. § 300.8 (2017). https://www.law.cornell.edu/cfr/text/34/300.8

7

January

The following principal leadership standards support your tasks for this month.

Box 7.1 2015 PSEL and Promoting Principal Leadership for the Success of Students with Disabilities

Effective principals ...

(4) implement valid monitoring and assessment systems.
(5) build a safe, caring, and healthy environment for students with disabilities that promotes inclusivity and opportunities to learn from their non-disabled peers to the greatest extent possible; and encourages them to be active, responsible members of their community.
(9) manage their budgets, school structures, operations, and systems; develop relationships with feeder and connecting schools to manage enrollment and curricular articulation to support students with disabilities.

Curriculum, Instruction, and Assessment

Local or State Administered Student Assessments
♦ If local midyear testing or state testing is occurring at this time, check with your CSE chairperson to confirm that meetings held to date on students regarding the *current* school year have been finalized.

DOI: 10.4324/9781003483045-10

Why Is This Important?

It is still possible to adjust IEPs if necessary for the current school year, and meetings may not have been necessary (remember the "Proposed Amendment to IEP Form Without a Committee Meeting"). As such, IEPs may not have been finalized yet with the new changes and updated in the SMS for viewing. You will need the most current list of accommodations in order to plan the testing schedules appropriately.

Communities of Student Care and Support

Student Transition to Middle/High School

♦ For students who are "moving up" to middle school or high school, are their respective guidance counselors invited to the annual review meetings?

Why Is This Important?

IDEA requires that by age 16, a student's IEP is developed to include transition planning (20 U.S.C. § 1401[34][A]), the purpose of which is to prepare students for postsecondary life. Given that students have the right to attend their CSE meetings (however, this is a parent/guardian decision based on factors such as the student's age and benefits to be gained from their attendance), having their guidance counselor present provides them with an excellent opportunity to discuss subjects and extracurricular areas of interest, and learn to advocate for themselves. They may have specific concerns, such as how to manage combination locks if they have fine motor or vision difficulties or getting to classes on time if they have mobility issues.

This can be a stressful time for many students, especially your students with IEPs or 504 plans given their respective challenges. Having their guidance counselor at the meeting to share information about courses and the daily schedule can help ease any apprehensions and provide them with a familiar face on day one.

Operations and Management

Testing Considerations

1. When reviewing test accommodations, especially for computer-based tests (CBT), it is quite possible that not all of the student's IEP accommodations (or 504) will match the state's list of allowable accommodations. Examine all entries for clarification, as some testing conditions noted may be unclear or omitted.

2. Computer-based state tests require the principal to enter the test accommodations into the system due to accountability concerns and the need to verify that the accommodations are correct. Entry errors could result in a misadministration report to the Office of Special Education (OSE).

3. Are faculty and support staff aware of CBT protocols? Professional development will ensure consistency among test administrators.

4. It would be a good idea to speak with your director of technology about running checks on the system to avoid a possible "crash" on test day. Also, CBT assessments have varied considerations such as network availability, Wi-Fi setup, and the availability of power cords/strips (unless students are using their Chromebooks and testing in class). Work with your director of technology to ensure all facets of test administration have been addressed from a technology standpoint.

5. NYS provides the manual *Testing Accommodations for Students with Disabilities: Policy and Tools to Guide Decision-Making and Implementation* (NYSED, 2023). Check if your state has a similar manual for reference.

6. Students are to receive their test accommodations for *all* tests; it is not selective. If a student refuses their accommodations, there is a specific form (usually in the test manual) that must be completed, and the parent/ guardian is to be notified.

7. If testing is occurring for your ELL students, note that some of those students may be "ELLs with a disability"

and require accommodations. They may also be taking multiple exams. For instance, in NYS, they could be scheduled for the NYS English as a Second Language Test (NYSESLAT) in two sections—Speaking; Listening, Reading, and Writing, as well as their grade 3–8 state assessments in English Language Arts (ELA), math, and/or science (the latter is grade dependent). April and May would be busy testing months for them. Speak with their ENL teacher if you have questions.

8. Has proctor training or training in administering test accommodations been provided to staff? Some districts may assign two proctors per room as a checks and balances to ensure appropriate monitoring of test protocols.

9. Do you know the process for managing exams and answer sheets for students in out-of-district or private placements?

Why Is This Important?

Assessments are just one tool in the educational process, but they are vital for providing insights, driving improvement, and ensuring that all students have the opportunity to succeed, so it is essential that the process is carried out with fidelity. In addition, the test data from students in out-of-district placements will *also* count toward your data in the state data bank (same as for disciplinary incidences). Knowing that, it is a good idea to touch base with the out-of-district school principal on instructional practices (or even disciplinary protocols) being used to share best practices.

Budget Preparation for September

◆ Do you know what your projected enrollment and staffing needs are for the different class and grade configurations (e.g., 1:12:1; 1:8:1, integrated co-teaching)?

◆ How many 1:1 aides or classroom aides are anticipated based on CSE projections?

◆ Do you know if there are projections for students in out-of-district placements to transition back to their home school?

◆ How many preschool students with a disability who are "Turning 5" are expected to transition through CSE?
◆ Are any students graduating in January or attending half-day?
◆ How much should be budgeted for Child Find activities?

Why Is This Important?

During this period, administrative meetings will cover topics such as staffing, programs, grade and course sections, potential retirements, etc. With annual reviews underway or soon to begin, the director of special education will most likely have met with their staff to discuss student needs in order to project class/course configurations and personnel for the upcoming school year.

Having the conversation with them at this point will give you an idea of what your special education program requirements may be, classroom and therapy rooms needed, office space, etc. Though these projections may shift given the outcome of CSE meetings, you will at least have a starting point to begin drafting your instructional and staffing needs for budget conversations with your administrative team. Given that you have been keeping tabs on your students through report cards, five-week progress reports, cohort meetings, and conversations with faculty, you are in a good position to begin preliminary scheduling.

Section 504 Review Meetings

◆ Are you the coordinator for your building?
◆ If not, do you have a list of meeting dates?

Why Is This Important?

If you are in charge of overseeing 504 plans, have you begun scheduling yearly review meetings? Some districts may choose to review on the student's birth date. In any case, be sure to check meeting dates to avoid overlapping with CSE meetings and sub coverage.

January Checklist

Did you ...

- ☐ follow up on any updates or clarifications to students' test accommodations in preparation for local or state testing?
- ☐ meet with your director of special education to discuss a middle/high school transition process, and obtain projected student needs, class configurations, related services, and staffing numbers for your building in order to begin drafting your budget?
- ☐ start scheduling 504 review meetings if you are the assigned Section 504 coordinator; if not, do you have a list of meetings to plan for?
- ☐ review the testing considerations and address any areas of need?

References

Individuals with Disabilities Education Act of 2004, 20 U.S.C. § 1401 (2019). https://sites.ed.gov/idea/statute-chapter-33/subchapter-i/1401/34

New York State Education Department. (2023). *Testing accommodations for students with disabilities: Policy and tools to guide decision-making and implementation.* New York State Education Department. https://www.nysed.gov/sites/default/files-programs/special-education/testing-accommodations-guide_0.pdf

8

February

The following principal leadership standards support your tasks for this month.

Box 8.1 2015 PSEL and Promoting Principal Leadership for the Success of Students With Disabilities

Effective principals …

(4) communicate high academic expectations for students with disabilities; use multi-tiered systems of support; implement valid monitoring and assessment systems; and ensure evidence-based, differentiated approaches to instruction.

(7) establish a sense of collective responsibility and mutual accountability for the success of students with disabilities.

(9) manage their budgets, school structures, operations, and administrative systems; and develop relationships with feeder and connecting schools for enrollment management and curricular articulation to support students with disabilities.

DOI: 10.4324/9781003483045-11

Curriculum, Instruction, and Assessment

Report Cards— End of 2nd Quarter
◆ Will the CSE consider retention?

Why Is This Important?
The role of the CSE is to determine the specially designed instruction a student needs, in addition to recommendations for accommodations, related services, participation in the general education setting, etc. The decision to retain is made at the building level by the school principal, parent/guardian, and classroom teacher. Depending on the school's practice, consultation with the school-based team such as your IST or CST (or a similar configuration) *may* occur. A review of the board of education policy on retention could reveal a caveat such as, students with disabilities are held to different promotion standards.

Retaining a student with an IEP can be a slippery slope. "It would be difficult for a school to successfully argue at a due process hearing that they provided a program of 'specially designed instruction ... to meet the unique needs of a child' while also acknowledging that they did not teach the child the information he needs to know, so they want to retain him" (Whitney, 2017, para. 5). If a CSE program review has yet to be scheduled, it should be, to determine sequential next steps to assist the student in making progress toward their goals and objectives (which may also need adjusting). Remember, the student is eligible to receive building-level supports and progress monitoring should be ongoing.

In addition to a focus on learning challenges and academic status, it is important to take a holistic view and look at underlying concomitant factors that may also be having a contributory effect on the student's school performance—absenteeism, any health issues, family dysfunction, impact of socioeconomic factors such as housing or food insecurity, etc. A comprehensive strategy incorporating parent/guardian input can make the difference in a student's learning outcomes.

Operations and Management

Summer School and Funding Considerations
◆ Is the district providing a summer school program for all students who meet the criteria?

Why Is This Important?
It is budget season, and of the many discussions, one will be to deliberate the availability of funds to house a summer school program. These monies can come from both district funds as well as Title 1 monies provided by the federal government, based on a funding formula, and dispersed to your district. Title 1 funds are used to support students who meet the criteria through targeted assistance (e.g., economically, disadvantaged children to close the achievement gap, ELLs, homelessness) or via whole school eligibility as determined by the district's free and reduced lunch numbers. Said funds can be used to help support an AIS summer school for all students who are eligible based on the predetermined criteria.

Note that students with disabilities who require special education support during the summer to prevent substantial regression and are recommended for an extended school year (ESY) program (e.g., a special education classroom-based program and/or the provision of related services) by the CSE are *not* eligible for enrollment in the district's summer school unless the school runs its own ESY program.

Child Find
◆ As noted in September, Child Find is a federal mandate under IDEA that requires schools to do outreach to the community for the purpose of identifying children in need of special education attention.

Why Is This Important?
To address responsibilities in this area, school districts are required to set aside funds to develop outreach activities. Examples of said activities can include notification via the school

website, social media channels, creating a school brochure that includes information about Child Find and the evaluation process, etc. Confer with the director of special education to coordinate activities and financial allocations in the school budget.

Are Students Returning from Out-of-District Placements?

◆ This is the time of year when the director of special education, and possibly business manager, will meet with their BOCES counterpart (if in NYS) or with administrative staff in other CSE recommended day or residential placements to discuss students' projected service needs for September.

Why Is This Important?

Every year the discussion is had as to whether students can successfully return to a program in district. Sometimes you have enough students to create a suitable class and sometimes you don't. If the district were able to create a class, but did not have enough students to fill it, they could inquire if surrounding districts also had the need and were willing to pay tuition for their student/s to attend. From a planning perspective, this is a conversation that you and the director of special education will have given the logistics involved.

February Checklist

Did you ...

- [ ] follow up on student concerns, inquire if a CSE program review has been scheduled or what the outcome was, and if building-level supports have been implemented?
- [ ] inquire about the status of summer school?
- [ ] discuss Child Find responsibilities and budgetary allocations with the director of special education, as well as the possibility of students returning to their home school from an out-of-district placement?

Reference

Whitney, S. (2017). Doing your homework: Retention! Special ed. teacher needs ammunition. Wrightslaw. https://www.wrightslaw.com/heath/teach.retain.htm

Part IV
Third Quarter Marking Period

9

March

The following principal leadership standards support your tasks for this month.

Box 9.1 2015 PSEL and Promoting Principal Leadership for the Success of Students with Disabilities

Effective principals …

(4) communicate high academic expectations for students with disabilities; develop teacher capacity for effective instruction; use multi-tiered systems of support; implement valid monitoring and assessment systems; ensure evidence-based, differentiated approaches to instruction; and implement technology for teaching and learning.

(7) establish a sense of collective responsibility and mutual accountability for the success of students with disabilities.

(9) assign roles and responsibilities to optimize staff capacity to address each student's learning needs and manage school structures, operations, and systems to support students with disabilities.

DOI: 10.4324/9781003483045-13

Curriculum, Instruction, and Assessment

Five-Week Marking Period
+ Continue to follow up on students for whom teachers are expressing concerns.

Why Is This Important?
An initial CSE referral may be in process for students who have received the continuum of supports yet academic challenges persist.

For students with IEPs, CSE program reviews may be ongoing to tweak the IEP based on specific areas of concern. Have interventions through MTSS been applied, such as the provision of socio-emotional support, peer mentoring, Check-in/ Check-out, etc.? Is additional professional development needed for teachers on new resources? Have supplementary services been considered, such as after-school tutoring? ESY is generally discussed at the annual review. Conversations should be occurring with the student to discuss learning preferences, goals, and the support they feel they need. There is a lot to consider.

Conversely, there is a saying about "throwing Jello at the wall to see what sticks." And while it is natural and absolutely well-intentioned to explore multiple options to help students, it is also essential to be strategic about the process, determine the specific targets to focus on, regularly monitor the outcomes, evaluate, and build from there in progressive steps.

Operations and Management

NYS Report of Personnel Employed or Contracted to Provide Special Education and Related Services to Students with Disabilities (PD-6)
+ Your special education students are provided services by a variety of individuals. Do you know who they are?

Why Is This Important?
In NYS, the PD-6 report is due this month and is completed online by your director of special education. It includes the

names, certifications, licenses, and full-time equivalency (FTE) of all individuals providing the mandated supports to students as per their IEPs (e.g., special education teachers, paraprofessionals, related services personnel, social workers, medical/nursing staff, physical education teachers who are providing adaptive physical education, etc.). It may not be a complete list as BOCES (or a similar agency in your state) reports their own personnel even though your district may contract with them to provide a service (e.g., a physical therapist two days/week). However, if they cannot provide the service requested and the district needs to seek an independent provider to contract with, that person will be listed on the PD-6 form for you to identify.

It is understandable to assume that any special education services being provided to your students with disabilities are all being done by in district staff, but you might be incorrect. Reviewing this report with the director of special education is not only informative from a budgeting aspect, but also to know who is coming and going in your building, as well as the types of services required by your students with disabilities. Check to see if a similar report is available for review in your state.

Substitute Coverage

◆ Are you keeping updated on the coverage needs for your building?

Why Is This Important?

The list of substitutes in your district may be limited, and you need coverage for CSE meetings, 504 meetings, testing, and general staff absences. Continue to stay abreast of the situation in case issues arise.

Master Schedule—Special Education

Though by no means a comprehensive list, consider the following:

1. How many special education classes are projected?
2. How many integrated co-teaching classes are projected?
3. How are the special education teachers being assigned?

4. Do you know if students have been recommended to participate in a less restrictive setting for a particular class? Half the day? (You want to avoid an overlap of classes, which can prevent a student from accessing a required subject.)

5. Is co-teacher planning time built in?

6. How are you balancing the scheduling of intervention periods against classes and special area subjects to avoid an "either-or" scenario for students in terms of their ability to participate as needed?

7. Do core subjects have defined times of instruction (e.g., ELA and math in a.m. and science and social studies in p.m.) to enable students who are being considered for less restrictive or more restrictive placements the flexibility of doing so without missing another subject?

8. Which classes have support staff available?

Why Is This Important?

Though CSE meetings are ongoing, you should request a list of projected special education classes for your students in order to initiate the scheduling process. In addition, you have a preliminary plan of course needs based on enrollment and information obtained from the budget discussions that have occurred. Creating a schedule that meets students' IEP recommendations and ensures access to opportunities is quite the task given all of the components that need to be coordinated. Consider organizing a scheduling committee for input to help identify any obstacles, optimize staff resources, and brainstorm course conflict scenarios. Your guidance counselors are of assistance in this process, given their knowledge of grade-level courses and students. Be sure to include special education representatives as their insight regarding course scheduling and how students manage their day is important.

Planning for a Half-Day School and Vocational-Technology Schedule

◆ Do you know if students will be attending Vo-Tech in the morning or afternoon?

Why Is This Important?

Knowing the half day schedule of students is important for planning purposes. You may have students who are attending Vo-Tech and scheduled to graduate in January, but they have to repeat US History, and it has to be an integrated co-teaching class because that is their IEP recommended program. You will need to schedule that class for the fall, and a.m. or p.m. depending on the Vo-Tech bus schedule, which may have a domino effect on other courses. You should also note any factors that will influence scheduling (e.g., your history teacher may also be a coach who needs to leave early on game days; hence, their class should be in the morning, but dependent on the bus run).

March Checklist

Did you ...

- [ ] follow up with teachers regarding student concerns during this five-week marking period and inquire about the progressive steps being taken this far?
- [ ] review your sub coverage list against upcoming meetings?
- [ ] organize a committee for input on drafting the master schedule?
- [ ] follow up on students attending school half day from other sites?

Reference

New York State Education Department. (2020). *PD-6 report of personnel employed or contracted to provide special education and related services to students with disabilities.* https://www.p12.nysed.gov/sedcar/forms/pdforms/2021/pdf/pd6.pdf

10

April

The following principal leadership standards support your tasks for this month.

Box 10.1 2015 PSEL and Promoting Principal Leadership for the Success of Students with Disabilities

Effective principals …

(4) communicate high academic expectations for students with disabilities; develop teacher capacity for effective instruction; use multi-tiered systems of support; implement valid monitoring and assessment systems; ensure evidence-based, differentiated approaches to instruction; and promote the effective use of technology for teaching and learning.

(6) provide high-quality, meaningful, professional development to effectively educate students with disabilities.

(7) establish a sense of collective responsibility and mutual accountability for the success of students with disabilities.

(9) manage school structures, operations, and systems to support students with disabilities.

DOI: 10.4324/9781003483045-14

Curriculum, Instruction, and Assessment

Report Cards—End of 3rd Quarter

♦ By now, students in question should have either had their initial CSE meeting, with recommendations made, or their Program Review/s with amendments.

Questions to consider:

1. What progress is being made towards their IEP goals and objectives?
2. With regard to specially designed instruction, how has content, methodology, or delivery of instruction been adapted to meet the student's needs (34 C.F.R. § 300.39[b] [3])?
3. Are non-academic concerns being addressed?
4. How often is progress monitoring occurring?
5. Is the student showing regression after long weekends or school breaks?
6. In what specific areas of the curriculum is the student having difficulties?
7. Have parents been kept apprised of the issues and offered opportunities for input?
8. Is documentation of all meetings and parent conversations held to date being kept (e.g., in the SMS)?
9. Has an extended school day or school year (ESY) been recommended by the CSE?

Why Is This Important?

As noted in February, "It would be difficult for a school to successfully argue at a due process hearing that they provided a program of "specially designed instruction ... to meet the unique needs of a child while also acknowledging that they did not teach the child the information he needs to know, so they want to retain him" (Whitney, 2017, para. 5). It is critical to ensure that the specific areas of difficulty are being addressed and the IEP is amended as needed to meet the student's needs and build progress towards their goals and objectives.

Professional Capacity of School Personnel

Summer Professional Development

◆ Confer with the director of special education regarding joint opportunities for professional development specifically geared toward students with disabilities (e.g., strategies for behavior management, co-teaching models, understanding types of disabilities and best practices for instruction, inclusive practices).

Why Is This Important?

Planning ahead is key to maximizing your staff's expertise in leading workshops and professional development sessions unless an outside facilitator is being considered. Furthermore, integrating data from state special education reports can inspire collaboration among staff members to effectively address any areas of concern that are identified. This proactive approach can lead to impactful outcomes and positive developments in supporting students' needs.

Operations and Management

School/District Safety Plan—Students with Disabilities

◆ Does your school's safety plan include accommodations for students with disabilities?

Why Is This Important?

All schools have safety/crisis plans that cover a variety of topics such as active school shooter drills or emergency evacuations, but "few school plans address the complex needs of students with disabilities. School supports should include an analysis of school plans and student strengths and needs to ensure that students with disabilities have the best opportunity to be safe in a school crisis" (Clarke et al., 2014, p. 169). How do you plan for students with sensory processing deficits who are being triggered by the noise they hear or don't want to stay in the closet for safety because of a fear of tight spaces? Students who might elope? Students who are in a wheelchair or have crutches and the steps and elevator are unavailable for use? What about students who have health issues and need their medication? Who debriefs the incident with them afterward? Whether adding this review to the summer calendar or finding time for the school Crisis Team and/or SAVE and Wellness Committee to meet during school hours, a reevaluation of your plan with additions for how to include support for students with disabilities is necessary. Planned updates with a focus on inclusivity for students with disabilities are essential to ensure comprehensive and effective crisis management.

April Checklist

Did you ...

- [ ] follow up with teachers on outcomes of CSE initial referral meetings or program reviews for students of concern?
- [ ] confer with the director of special education regarding joint collaboration on the delivery of summer professional development for faculty and staff with a focus on special education?
- [ ] begin making arrangements for summer professional development?
- [ ] arrange for the school Crisis Team and/or SAVE/Wellness team to meet and review the school safety/crisis plan?

References

Clarke, L. S., Embury, D. C., Jones, R. E., & Yssel, N. (2014). Supporting students with disabilities during school crises: A teacher's guide. *Exceptional Children*, 46(6), 1–10. https://doi.org/10.1177/0040059914534616

IDEA Regulations, 34 C.F.R. § 300.39 (2024). https://www.ecfr.gov/current/title-34/subtitle-B/chapter-III/part-300/subpart-A/subject-group-ECFR0ec59c730ac278e/section-300.39

Whitney, S. (2017). *Doing your homework: Retention! Special ed. teacher needs ammunition*. Wrightslaw. https://www.wrightslaw.com/heath/teach.retain.htm

Part V

Final Quarter Marking Period

11

May

The following principal leadership standards support your tasks for this month.

Box 11.1 2015 PSEL and Promoting Principal Leadership for the Success of Students with Disabilities

Effective principals ...

(4) communicate high academic expectations for students with disabilities; use multi-tiered systems of support; implement valid monitoring and assessment systems; and ensure evidence-based, differentiated approaches to instruction for students with disabilities.

(5) provide students with disabilities opportunities to learn from their non-disabled peers to the greatest extent possible and encourages them to be active, responsible members of their community.

(8) establish a sense of collective responsibility and mutual accountability for the success of students with disabilities.

(9) manage their budgets and school structures, operations, and systems to support students with disabilities.

DOI: 10.4324/9781003483045-16

Curriculum, Instruction, and Assessment

Five Week Progress Reports—Summer School vs. Extended School Year

♦ If ESY was not discussed at the student's annual review meeting, this is a time when a CSE program review must be held to determine eligibility based on progress to date towards goals and objectives.

♦ Is summer school an option for participation?

Why Is This Important?

The CSE will determine whether ESY services are needed to provide FAPE (34 C.F.R. § 300.17) and whether the student will likely regress over the summer without the support and/or have difficulty recouping learned skills. If the district is offering summer school, students have equal opportunity to participate. As such, the district would continue to provide the supports and accommodations listed on their IEP. However, consideration needs to be given as to whether or not a general education summer school program is most appropriate if the student has been receiving specialized instruction during the school year in a special education classroom.

Communities of Student Care and Support

Transition Planning

♦ Inquire if your guidance counselors have met with eligible students to discuss employment, social, or volunteer opportunities during the summer months.

Why Is This Important?

Transition planning is not a one-time event. Under IDEA, students begin the transition planning process by age 16 at the latest, or earlier if deemed appropriate. The summer months provide an opportunity for students to pursue varied activities in areas of interest, attend summer camp to enhance socialization and skill building, or obtain employment. Beginning the conversation and exploration of opportunities at this time contributes to the intent of the process—self-discovery and independence.

Operations and Management

Master Schedule Update

◆ Have you requested a list of the most current CSE projections for September?

◆ Was a committee formed to provide input?

Why Is This Important?

The IEP outlines students' instructional programs, which makes it an important consideration when determining the master schedule. Since annual reviews are winding down at this point, you should have a realistic idea of your classes and programs given the updated list of projections.

Having a committee provide suggestions from a "boots on the ground" perspective is invaluable as you navigate the many factors involved in creating the schedule, which, at this point, should be in draft form with final revisions occurring in June if needed.

Declassification Support Services

◆ In NYS, students who have been declassified following updated testing may be recommended for declassification support services (DSS). The purpose of this is to provide a transition to general education without support by the end of the school year (20 U.S.C. § 1400 et seq.).

◆ Services recommended may consist of options like testing accommodations, instructional modifications, or related services; however, the student will *not* have an IEP.

◆ This option may or may not be available in your state. Contact the director of special education for further information.

Why Is This Important?

These students still have the right to their recommended services for one year despite not having an IEP and said services may have an impact on class configurations. Request a list of students to ensure that any recommendations are carried out come September. Inquire about the process for notifying teachers, as these students will still require monitoring. It could be that DSS are flagged (color-coded) in your student management system for one year and then automatically dropped. At any rate, teachers will need to know how to access the declassification plans.

Planning for Graduation

♦ Do you have a list of your classified high school students who are graduating?

♦ Does this list also include students who were placed in out-of-district settings as per CSE recommendations?

♦ Do you know what type of diploma and/or certificate they earned (in addition to any attached seals and endorsements to the NYS assigned diploma)?

♦ Are your out-of-district students planning on attending graduation at their home school?

♦ Have they been invited to participate in end-of-year senior class activities (e.g., class trip, prom, dances, recognition nights), and are any supports needed to enable their participation (e.g., aides)?

Why Is This Important?

Students who have been placed in programs out of district as per the CSE also have the right to attend their home school graduation; therefore, check that all information pertaining to graduating seniors has been forwarded. If they choose to graduate with their class in their out-of-district placement, follow up to confirm that their diploma and/or certificate was forwarded to the school principal at that site, unless the process is to mail them home.

Your guidance counselors should have a list of students who are on track for graduation at this time. Verify the list with the director of special education so as to order the correct documents and certificates.

Individuals with Disabilities Education Act—Part B Sections 611 and 619 Grants

◆ Do you have additional program needs for your students with disabilities or special education staff that were not originally factored in when completing your budget?

Why Is This Important?

The Office of Special Education Programs (OSEP) oversees IDEA grants, which are formula-based and used to cover the excess costs of providing special education and related services to students with disabilities in grades PreK–12. Part B 611 serves students ages 6–21, and 619 focuses on preschool services for children ages 3–5. The director of special education has options for allocating these funds, such as for professional development, assistive technology, contracted special education services, aides, and more. Although their allocations may already be set, it is well worth the conversation. The deadline is usually July 1 for submission.

May Checklist

Did you ...

☐ inquire if a determination has been made of students recommended for ESY?

☐ develop the list of students eligible to attend the district's summer school program, and are any students with disabilities included?

☐ inquire if the guidance counselors began summer transition planning for eligible high school students?

☐ finish drafting the master schedule?

☐ arrange for co-teacher planning time—either before the end of the year or in the summer?

☐ obtain a list of students who have declassification support services?

☐ request a list of students on track to graduate next month (including from out-of-district CSE recommended placements) along with a determination of the type of diploma and/or certificate earned?

☐ confer with the director of special education regarding possible service needs under the IDEA Section 611 (and possibly 619) grants?

References

IDEA Regulations, 34 C.F.R. § 300.17 (2017). https://sites.ed.gov/idea/regs/b/a/300.17

Individuals with Disabilities Education Act of 2004, 20 U.S.C. § 1400 et seq. (2010). https://www.law.cornell.edu/uscode/text/20/1400

June

The following principal leadership standards support your tasks for this month.

Box 12.1 2015 PSEL and Promoting Principal Leadership for the Success of Students with Disabilities

Effective principals …

(4) communicate high academic expectations for students with disabilities.

(7) establish collective responsibility and mutual accountability for the success of students with disabilities.

(9) manage school structures, operations, and systems to support students with disabilities.

Curriculum, Instruction, and Assessment

Report Cards—End of 4th Quarter

♦ Meeting the diverse needs of students and ensuring their progress towards their individual goals and objectives demands a collaborative, personalized, progressive, and adaptable approach involving educators, students, families, and the wider school community.

DOI: 10.4324/9781003483045-17

Why Is This Important?

"A century of research has failed to demonstrate the benefits of grade retention over promotion for *any* group of students. The focus must be on implementing evidence-based prevention and intervention strategies to promote social and cognitive competence and facilitate the academic success of *all* students" (Anderson et al., 2002, p. 2).

The IEP is designed to "meet the child's needs that result from the child's disability to enable the child to be involved in and make progress in the general education curriculum" (34 C.F.R. § 320). By strategically implementing a variety of interventions and instructional strategies such as the inclusion of related services, frequent progress monitoring, adjusting accommodations and modifications as needed, adding building level interventions (e.g., AIS, RTI, or MTSS), scheduling CSE program reviews, modifying the IEP, incorporating specialized instruction, the addition of supplemental supports (extended day for intensive tutoring, and/or ESY), and assuming a student-centered approach, progress can be achieved.

Operations and Management

Master Schedule, Room Facilitation, and Class Assignments

◆ Have your special education class lists been determined, including integrated co-teaching?

◆ Are co-teaching planning periods built into the schedule?

◆ Do you have a list of classified students from the office of special education to check against your class lists, as well as a list of students who have declassification support services?

◆ Do you have a list of students who have 504 plans?

◆ Do you know which support staff have been assigned as 1:1 aides or classroom aides based on IEP recommendations?

◆ Do you know of any specific room placements that need to be addressed?

◆ Do you have students entering from out of district settings?

Why Is This Important?

Sometimes there is a glitch, and the lists between the principal's office and the office of special education don't align; this may be due to delays in finalizing IEPs. Reviewing both sets of class lists will help identify if all students are accounted for.

It is important to strategically assign aides and organize class sections to maximize support for students with specific needs. By reviewing aide assignments and class enrollments, you can better determine how to provide the necessary accommodations. For example, placing students with similar accommodations together (e.g., test read) with existing support staff in the classroom (teacher aide/assistant vs 1:1) can enhance their learning experience and ensure they receive the assistance they need. This approach can create a more inclusive and supportive learning environment for students.

Room facilitation issues may cause some concerns when you are trying to group class sections together, but you need to be aware of IEP notations such as, "requires bathroom access in the classroom," or "proximity to nurse's office." Speak with the CSE chairperson or director of special education if you have any questions.

Graduation Planning Follow-Up

♦ Have there been any changes to the list of students who are graduating?

♦ Consult the director of special education regarding students' in out-of-district placements and their attendance at graduation. Are they choosing to attend one or both ceremonies?

♦ If students are attending both ceremonies, are arrangements made for them to participate in the rehearsal at their home school? Did they order their cap and gown?

♦ If they decide to attend the ceremony at their current school, have the necessary diplomas/certificates been forwarded to their school principals (or is the practice to have them mailed, and you just provide the diploma cover for the ceremony)?

Why Is This Important?
Confirming the nuances involved with graduation planning will ensure a seamless and well-deserved commencement day for all seniors and their families.

Summer School and/or Extended School Year Programs
♦ Do you know who your students are?
♦ Will planning time be allotted before the end of the year for teachers assigned to summer school (or ESY if being held in district)?

Why Is This Important?
Whether you are holding summer school and/or an extended school year program in district, student lists should be developed by this time and parents/guardians notified. The extended school year program would generally be under the guidance of the director of special education, but you should be aware of the students in session and program overview.

Teachers of both programs should be allotted time to meet and discuss how to structure the weeks of service delivery (e.g., how to differentiate instruction to address the diverse learning styles, effective classroom management, assessments to monitor progress, materials required, etc.). In addition, summer school teachers will need to be aware of students who have IEPs as their accommodations and supports remain in effect to enable students to access the program in place.

Collection of Assistive Technology Equipment
♦ Has equipment assigned to students been collected, labeled with the student's name, and returned to either the office of special education or principal's office for placement in storage?
♦ Are any students keeping their equipment for summer use in their ESY or summer school program?

Why Is This Important?
Assistive technology equipment is purchased by the school for student use (or borrowed from a lending library). Notification

should be sent to teachers and related services providers informing them of the process for returning equipment; this can be managed by the office of special education or you. Defer to the director of special education for how equipment is being managed during summer months if in use by students or dispersed in September.

Academic Services Team Meeting

◆ Arrange a time to meet with your AIS, RTI, and MTSS providers.

Why Is This Important?

School principals play a critical role in ensuring that all students receive an equitable education. By evaluating the academic intervention programs with providers, you can engage in collaborative discussions to assess what worked well and identify areas for improvement to align practices and enhance service delivery for students. Questions to consider include program capacity, the range of students' needs, the number of repeat students in the programs and why, potential barriers to students' success, and entry/exit criteria. Moreover, the classification of a learning disability requires adherence to RTI protocols and scientific research-based interventions before formal consideration. Having established processes in place ensures accurate identification of needs and informed decision-making to secure equitable access, where every student has the opportunity to excel in school, regardless of their background or circumstances . . . all in preparation for a new school year.

June Checklist

Did you …

- [ ] finalize the master schedule?
- [ ] obtain a list of special classes and assignments for special education faculty and support staff?
- [ ] obtain a list of room facilitation concerns to assist with planning class placements?
- [ ] confirm that diplomas and/or certificates for graduating students who have chosen to attend the ceremony at their CSE recommended out-of-district placements have been sent to the school principals?
- [ ] confirm that you have all diplomas and/or certificates for students with disabilities who are graduating in district?
- [ ] finalize student lists for summer school and/or the ESY program if being held in district?
- [ ] follow up on the process for collecting and/or distributing assistive technology equipment to students who have the accommodation and are attending summer school or the ESY program?
- [ ] schedule a school-based interventions team meeting to discuss program effectiveness and make adjustments for September?

References

Anderson, E., Whipple, A. D., & Jimerson, S. R. (2002). *Grade retention: Achievement and mental health outcomes.* National Association of School Psychologists. https://www.wrightslaw.com/info/fape. grade.retention.nasp.pdf

IDEA Regulations, 34 C.F.R § 300.320 (2017). https://www.sites.ed.gov/ idea/regs/b/d/300.320/a

Appendix A

Master Calendar for the Year

July

Communities of Student Care and Support
Individual Education Program—Special Alerts
Professional Capacity of School Personnel
Professional Development Plans
Operations and Management
Summer School Preparation
Assistive Technology Needs
New Entrants Transitioning from Services under the Committee on Preschool Education
Student Enrollment and Integrated Co-Teaching Ratios
Responsibilities of Teacher Aides and Teacher Assistants in Special Education
Transfer Students with an IEP or 504 Plan
Student Management System—Access To IEPs and 504 Plans
New York State School Safety and Educational Climate Report

August

Equity and Cultural Responsiveness
English Language Learners With a Handicapping Condition
Student Test Data and English Language Learners With/Without Disabilities
Discipline—IDEA vs. State Regulations
Home Instruction

Communities of Student Care and Support
School Nurse Responsibility
Professional Community for Teachers and Staff
Case Managers
Meaningful Engagement of Families and Community
Home-School Communication for Non-English-Speaking Parents/Guardians
Operations and Management
Integrated Co-Teacher Planning Time
Review Class Lists
Student Management System—IEP/504 Access and Communication Log
Bus Driver/Bus Monitor Training
Section 504
Individuals with Disabilities Education Act
School Improvement
State Performance Plan for Federal Indicators

September

Ethics and Professional Norms
Confidentiality of IEPs and 504 Plans
Curriculum, Instruction, and Assessment
Local Student Assessments
Communities of Student Care and Support
Assistive Technology- School Website and LOTE
Professional Capacity of School Personnel
Special Education Teacher Evaluations
Professional Community for Teachers and Staff
Cohort Meetings for Student Monitoring
Case Manager Follow-Up
Meaningful Engagement of Families and Communities
Child Find Responsibilities
Operations and Management
Transfer Students with an IEP or 504 Plan
State Assessment Preparation
McKinney-Vento Homeless Assistance Act

October

Curriculum, Instruction, and Assessment
> Five-Week Progress Reports
> Monitor Assistive Technology

Operations and Management
> Transfer Students with an IEP or 504 Plan
> Classroom Student Groupings and Service Provision

School Improvement
> NYS Verification Report 2—School Age Child Count by Age and Disability
> NYS Verification Report 3—School Age Students by Disability and Race/Ethnicity
> NYS Verification Report 5—School Age Least Restrictive Environment Setting
> NYS Verification Report 8—District Report of School-Age Students by Building of Enrollment

November

Curriculum, Instruction, and Assessment
> Report Cards—End of 1st Quarter
> Progress Monitoring

Operations and Management
> Class Lists and Support Staff Update

December

Curriculum, Instruction, and Assessment
> Five-Week Progress Reports

Operations and Management
> Assistive Technology Plan
> General Annual Review/CSE Meeting Guidance
> Kindergarten Entrants Transitioning from the Committee on Preschool Education
> Substitute Coverage and Annual Review Planning

January

Curriculum, Instruction, and Assessment
Local or State Administered Student Assessments
Communities of Student Care and Support
Student Transition to Middle/High School
Operations and Management
Testing Considerations
Budget Preparation for September
Section 504 Review Meetings

February

Curriculum, Instruction, and Assessment
Report Cards—End of 2nd Quarter
Operations and Management
Summer School and Funding Considerations
Child Find
Are Students Returning From Out-of-District Placements?

March

Curriculum, Instruction, and Assessment
Five-Week Marking Period
Operations and Management
NYS Report of Personnel Employed or Contracted to Provide
    Special Education and Related Services to Students with
    Disabilities (PD-6)
Substitute Coverage
Master Schedule—Special Education
Planning for a Half-Day School and Vocational-Technology
    Schedule

April

Curriculum, Instruction, and Assessment
Report Cards—End of 3rd Quarter

Professional Capacity of School Personnel
Summer Professional Development
Operations and Management
School/District Safety Plan—Students with Disabilities

May

Curriculum, Instruction, and Assessment
Five-Week Progress Reports—Summer School vs. Extended
School Year
Communities of Student Care and Support
Transition Planning
Operations and Management
Master Schedule Update
Declassification Support Services
Planning for Graduation
Individuals with Disabilities Education Act—Part B Sections
611 and 619 Grants

June

Curriculum, Instruction, and Assessment
Report Cards—End of 4th Quarter
Operations and Management
Master Schedule, Room Facilitation, and Class Assignments
Graduation Planning Follow-Up
Summer School and/or Extended School Year Programs
Collection of Assistive Technology Equipment
Academic Services Team Meeting

Appendix B

List of Abbreviations and Acronyms

504	Section 504 of the Rehabilitation Act of 1973
AIS	Academic Intervention Services
ARD	Admission, Review and Dismissal team
BEDS	Basic Education Data System
BLT	Building Leadership Team
BOCES	Board of Cooperative Education Services
BOE	Board of Education
CCSSO	Council of Chief State School Officers
Co-Ser	Cooperative Services
CPSE	Committee on Preschool Special Education
CRDC	Civil Rights Data Collection
CSE	Committee on Special Education
CST	Child Study Team
DASA	Dignity for All Students Act
DSS	Declassified Support Services
ED	Emotional Disability
EIT	Electronic Information Technology
ELL	English Language Learner
ENL	English as a New Language
ESSA	Every Student Succeeds Act
ESY	Extended School Year
FAPE	Free Appropriate Public Education
FERPA	Family Educational Rights and Privacy Act
FM	Frequency Modulation
IDEA	Individuals with Disabilities Education Act
IDEIA	Individuals with Disabilities Education Improvement Act
IEE	Independent Education Evaluation

IEP	Individualized Education Program
IST	Instructional Support Team
LOTE	Language Other Than English
LRE	Least Restrictive Environment
MTSS	Multi-Tiered System of Supports
NYS	New York State
NYSED	NYS Education Department
NYSESLAT	NYS English as a Second Language Achievement Test
OCR	Office of Civil Rights
OHI	Other Health Impairment
OSE	Office of Special Education
OSEP	Office of Special Education Programs
OSERS	Office of Special Education and Rehabilitative Services
PBIS	Positive Behavioral Interventions and Supports
PD-6	Priority Date—NYS Report of Personnel Employed or Needed to Provide Special Education and Related Services to Students with Disabilities
PE	Physical Education
PSD	Preschool Student with a Disability
PSEL	Professional Standards for Educational Leaders
PTA	Parent Teacher Association
PWN	Prior Written Notice
RTI	Response to Intervention
SAVE	Safe Schools Against Violence in Education
SESIR	School Environmental Safety Incident Reporting
SLD	Specific Learning Disability
SMS	Student Management System
SSEC	School Safety and Educational Climate
VADIR	Violence and Disruptive Incident Report
Vo-Tech	Vocational Technology
VR	Verification Report

Appendix C

Internet Resources

National Center for Learning Disabilities, *Understand the Issues* (IDEA, 504, ESSA, ADA)	https://www.ncld.org
Section 508 of the Rehabilitation Act	https://www.section508.gov
U.S. Department of Education Office for Civil Rights	https://www2.ed.gov/ocr
U.S. Department of Education Office for Civil Rights, *Transition of Students with Disabilities to Postsecondary Education: A Guide for Educators*	https://www2.ed.gov/about/offices/list/ocr/transitionguide.html
Getting to Know New York State's Performance Plan/Annual Report	https://www.nysed.gov/sites/default/files/programs/special-education/state-performance-plan-overview-handout.pdf